California
HMH SCIENCE DIMENSIONS™
Volume 2

Grade 6
Units 3–4

Watch the cover come alive as you explore the body systems of a snail.
Download the HMH Science Dimensions AR app available on Android or iOS devices.

This Write-In Book belongs to

_____

Teacher/Room

_____

Houghton Mifflin Harcourt™

Consulting Authors

Michael A. DiSpezio

Global Educator
North Falmouth,
Massachusetts

Michael DiSpezio has authored many HMH instructional programs for Science and Mathematics. He has also authored numerous trade books and multimedia programs on various topics and hosted dozens of studio and location broadcasts for various organizations in the United States and worldwide. Most recently, he has been working with educators to provide strategies for implementing the Next Generation Science Standards, particularly the Science and Engineering Practices, Crosscutting Concepts, and the use of Evidence Notebooks. To all his projects, he brings his extensive background in science, his expertise in classroom teaching at the elementary, middle, and high school levels, and his deep experience in producing interactive and engaging instructional materials.

Marjorie Frank

Science Writer and Content-Area Reading Specialist
Brooklyn, New York

An educator and linguist by training, a writer and poet by nature, Marjorie Frank has authored and designed a generation of instructional materials in all subject areas, including past HMH Science programs. Her other credits include authoring science issues of an award-winning children's magazine, writing game-based digital assessments, developing blended learning materials for young children, and serving as instructional designer and coauthor of pioneering school-to-work software. In addition, she has served on the adjunct faculty of Hunter, Manhattan, and Brooklyn Colleges, teaching courses in science methods, literacy, and writing. For *California HMH Science Dimensions™*, she has guided the development of our K–2 strands and our approach to making connections between NGSS and Common Core ELA/literacy standards.

Acknowledgments

Cover credits: (garden snail) ©Johan Swanepoel/Alamy; (poison dart frog) ©Dirk Ercken/Alamy.

Section Header Master Art: (machinations) ©DNY59/E+/Getty Images; (rivers on top of Greenland ice sheet) ©Maria-José Viñas, NASA Earth Science News Team; (human cells, illustration) ©Sebastian Kaulitzki/Science Photo Library/Corbis; (waves) ©Alfred Pasieka/Science Source

Printed in the U.S.A.

ISBN 978-0-358-22118-0

4 5 6 7 8 9 10 0877 27 26 25 24 23 22

4500844122   B C D E F G

Michael R. Heithaus, PhD

Dean, College of Arts, Sciences & Education Professor, Department of Biological Sciences
Florida International University
Miami, Florida

Mike Heithaus joined the FIU Biology Department in 2003 and has served as Director of the Marine Sciences Program and Executive Director of the School of Environment, Arts, and Society, which brings together the natural and social sciences and humanities to develop solutions to today's environmental challenges. He now serves as Dean of the College of Arts, Sciences & Education. His research focuses on predator-prey interactions and the ecological importance of large marine species. He has helped to guide the development of Life Science content in *California HMH Science Dimensions™*, with a focus on strategies for teaching challenging content as well as the science and engineering practices of analyzing data and using computational thinking.

Bernadine Okoro

Access and Equity Consultant

S.T.E.M. Learning Advocate & Consultant
Washington, DC

Bernadine Okoro is a chemical engineer by training and a playwright, novelist, director, and actress by nature. Okoro went from working with patents and biotechnology to teaching in K–12 classrooms. A 12-year science educator and Albert Einstein Distinguished Fellow, Okoro was one of the original authors of the Next Generation Science Standards. As a member of the Diversity and Equity Team, her focus on Alternative Education and Community Schools and on Integrating Social-Emotional Learning and Brain-Based Learning into NGSS is the vehicle she uses as a pathway to support underserved groups from elementary school to adult education. An article and book reviewer for NSTA and other educational publishing companies, Okoro currently works as a S.T.E.M. Learning Advocate & Consultant.

Cary I. Sneider, PhD

Associate Research Professor
Portland State University
Portland, Oregon

While studying astrophysics at Harvard, Cary Sneider volunteered to teach in an Upward Bound program and discovered his real calling as a science teacher. After teaching middle and high school science in Maine, California, Costa Rica, and Micronesia, he settled for nearly three decades at Lawrence Hall of Science in Berkeley, California, where he developed skills in curriculum development and teacher education. Over his career, Cary directed more than 20 federal, state, and foundation grant projects and was a writing team leader for the Next Generation Science Standards. He has been instrumental in ensuring *California HMH Science Dimensions™* meets the high expectations of the NGSS and provides an effective three-dimensional learning experience for all students.

Program Advisors

Paul D. Asimow, PhD
Eleanor and John R. McMillan
Professor of Geology and
Geochemistry
California Institute of Technology
Pasadena, California

Joanne Bourgeois
Professor Emerita
Earth & Space Sciences
University of Washington
Seattle, WA

Dr. Eileen Cashman
Professor
Humboldt State University
Arcata, California

Elizabeth A. De Stasio, PhD
Raymond J. Herzog Professor of
Science
Lawrence University
Appleton, Wisconsin

Perry Donham, PhD
Lecturer
Boston University
Boston, Massachusetts

Shila Garg, PhD
Professor Emerita of Physics
Former Dean of Faculty & Provost
The College of Wooster
Wooster, Ohio

Tatiana A. Krivosheev, PhD
Professor of Physics
Clayton State University
Morrow, Georgia

Mark B. Moldwin, PhD
Professor of Space Sciences and
Engineering
University of Michigan
Ann Arbor, Michigan

Ross H. Nehm
Stony Brook University (SUNY)
Stony Brook, NY

Kelly Y. Neiles, PhD
Assistant Professor of Chemistry
St. Mary's College of Maryland
St. Mary's City, Maryland

John Nielsen-Gammon, PhD
Regents Professor
Department of Atmospheric
Sciences
Texas A&M University
College Station, Texas

Dr. Sten Odenwald
Astronomer
NASA Goddard Spaceflight Center
Greenbelt, Maryland

Bruce W. Schafer
Executive Director
Oregon Robotics Tournament &
Outreach Program
Beaverton, Oregon

Barry A. Van Deman
President and CEO
Museum of Life and Science
Durham, North Carolina

Kim Withers, PhD
Assistant Professor
Texas A&M University-Corpus
Christi
Corpus Christi, Texas

Adam D. Woods, PhD
Professor
California State University,
Fullerton
Fullerton, California

English Development Advisors

Mercy D. Momary
Local District Northwest
Los Angeles, California

Michelle Sullivan
Balboa Elementary
San Diego, California

Lab Safety Reviewer

Kenneth R. Roy, Ph.D.
Senior Lab Safety Compliance Consultant
National Safety Consultants, LLC
Vernon, Connecticut

Classroom Reviewers & Hands-On Activities Advisors

Julie Arreola
Sun Valley Magnet School
Sun Valley, California

Pamela Bluestein
Sycamore Canyon School
Newbury Park, California

Andrea Brown
HLPUSD Science & STEAM TOSA
Hacienda Heights, California

Stephanie Greene
Science Department Chair
Sun Valley Magnet School
Sun Valley, California

Rana Mujtaba Khan
Will Rogers High School
Van Nuys, California

Suzanne Kirkhope
Willow Elementary and Round
Meadow Elementary
Agoura Hills, California

George Kwong
Schafer Park Elementary
Hayward, California

Imelda Madrid
Bassett St. Elementary School
Lake Balboa, California

Susana Martinez O'Brien
Diocese of San Diego
San Diego, California

Craig Moss
Mt. Gleason Middle School
Sunland, California

Isabel Souto
Schafer Park Elementary
Hayward, California

Emily R.C.G. Williams
South Pasadena Middle School
South Pasadena, California

Flash floods can occur suddenly after a heavy rainfall. A lot of energy is released during a flash flood.

Foggy summer mornings in San Francisco happen as water from the Pacific Ocean evaporates into the air and then condenses. Wind carries the foggy air over land.

VOLUME 3

UNIT 5 Environmental and Genetic Influence on Organisms

379

This plumage display of a male bird of paradise attracts the female. With their needs met by the rich tropical rain forest, birds of paradise can spend extra time and energy on reproduction.

A lot of plastic trash ends up in the oceans, where it affects many organisms, such as plankton, corals, fish, and whales.

Claims, Evidence, and Reasoning

Constructing an Argument

Constructing a strong argument is useful in science and engineering and in everyday life. A strong argument has three parts: a claim, evidence, and reasoning. Scientists and engineers use claims-evidence-reasoning arguments to communicate their explanations and solutions to others and to challenge or debate the conclusions of other scientists and engineers. The words *argue* and *argument* do not mean that scientists or engineers are fighting about something. Instead, this is a way to support a claim using evidence. Argumentation is a calm and rational way for people to examine all the facts and come to the best conclusion.

A **claim** is a statement that answers the question "What do you know?" A claim is a statement of your understanding of a phenomenon, answer to a question, or solution to a problem. A claim states what you think is true based on the information you have.

Evidence is any data that are related to your claim and answer the question "How do you know that?" These data may be from your own experiments and observations, reports by scientists or engineers, or other reliable data. Arguments made in science and engineering should be supported by empirical evidence. Empirical evidence is evidence that comes from observation or experiment.

Evidence used to support a claim should also be relevant and sufficient. Relevant evidence is evidence that is about the claim, and not about something else. Evidence is sufficient when there is enough evidence to fully support the claim.

Reasoning is the use of logical, analytical thought to form conclusions or inferences. Reasoning answers the question "Why does your evidence support your claim?" So, reasoning explains the relationship between your evidence and your claim. Reasoning might include a scientific law or principle that helps explain the relationship between the evidence and the claim.

Here is an example of a claims-evidence-reasoning argument.

Claim	Ice melts faster in the sun than it does in the shade.
Evidence	Two ice cubes of the same size were each placed in a plastic dish. One dish was placed on a wooden bench in the sun and one was placed on a different part of the same bench in the shade. The ice cube in the sun melted in 14 minutes and 32 seconds. The ice cube in the shade melted in 18 minutes and 15 seconds.
Reasoning	This experiment was designed so that the only variable that was different in the set-up of the two ice cubes was whether they were in the shade or in the sun. Because the ice cube in the sun melted almost 4 minutes faster than the one in the shade, this is sufficient evidence to say that ice melts faster in the sun than it does in the shade.

To summarize, a strong argument:

- presents a claim that is clear, logical, and well-defended
- supports the claim with empirical evidence that is sufficient and relevant
- includes reasons that make sense and are presented in a logical order

Constructing Your Own Argument

Now construct your own argument by recording a claim, evidence, and reasoning. With your teacher's permission, you can do an investigation to answer a question you have about how the world works. Or you can construct your argument based on observations you have already made about the world.

Claim	
Evidence	
Reasoning	

For more information on claims, evidence, and reasoning, see the online **English Language Arts Handbook.**

Whether you are in the lab or in the field, you are responsible for your own safety and the safety of others. To fulfill these responsibilities and avoid accidents, be aware of the safety of your classmates as well as your own safety at all times. Take your lab work and fieldwork seriously, and behave appropriately. Elements of safety to keep in mind are shown below and on the following pages.

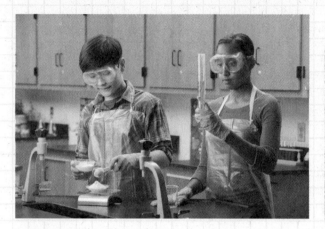

Safety in the Lab

- [ ] Be sure you understand the materials, your procedure, and the safety rules before you start an investigation in the lab.

- [ ] Know where to find and how to use fire extinguishers, eyewash stations, shower stations, and emergency power shutoffs.

- [ ] Use proper safety equipment. Always wear personal protective equipment, such as eye protection and gloves, when setting up labs, during labs, and when cleaning up.

- [ ] Do not begin until your teacher has told you to start. Follow directions.

- [ ] Keep the lab neat and uncluttered. Clean up when you are finished. Report all spills to your teacher immediately. Watch for slip/fall and trip/fall hazards.

- [ ] If you or another student is injured in any way, tell your teacher immediately, even if the injury seems minor.

- [ ] Do not take any food or drink into the lab. Never take any chemicals out of the lab.

Safety in the Field

- [ ] Be sure you understand the goal of your fieldwork and the proper way to carry out the investigation before you begin fieldwork.

- [ ] Use proper safety equipment and personal protective equipment, such as eye protection, that suits the terrain and the weather.

- [ ] Follow directions, including appropriate safety procedures as provided by your teacher.

- [ ] Do not approach or touch wild animals. Do not touch plants unless instructed by your teacher to do so. Leave natural areas as you found them.

- [ ] Stay with your group.

- [ ] Use proper accident procedures, and let your teacher know about a hazard in the environment or an accident immediately, even if the hazard or accident seems minor.

Safety Symbols

To highlight specific types of precautions, the following symbols are used throughout the lab program. Remember that no matter what safety symbols you see within each lab, all safety rules should be followed at all times.

Dress Code

- Wear safety goggles (or safety glasses as appropriate for the activity) at all times in the lab as directed. If chemicals get into your eye, flush your eyes immediately for a minimum of 15 minutes.
- Do not wear contact lenses in the lab.
- Do not look directly at the sun or any intense light source or laser.
- Wear appropriate protective non-latex gloves as directed.
- Wear an apron or lab coat at all times in the lab as directed.
- Tie back long hair, secure loose clothing, and remove loose jewelry. Remove acrylic nails when working with active flames.
- Do not wear open-toed shoes, sandals, or canvas shoes in the lab.

Glassware and Sharp Object Safety

- Do not use chipped or cracked glassware.
- Use heat-resistant glassware for heating or storing hot materials.
- Notify your teacher immediately if a piece of glass breaks.
- Use extreme care when handling any sharp or pointed instruments.
- Do not cut an object while holding the object unsupported in your hands. Place the object on a suitable cutting surface, and always cut in a direction away from your body.

Chemical Safety

- If a chemical gets on your skin, on your clothing, or in your eyes, rinse it immediately for a minimum of 15 minutes (using the shower, faucet, or eyewash station), and alert your teacher.
- Do not clean up spilled chemicals unless your teacher directs you to do so.
- Do not inhale any gas or vapor unless directed to do so by your teacher. If you are instructed to note the odor of a substance, wave the fumes toward your nose with your hand. This is called wafting. Never put your nose close to the source of the odor.
- Handle materials that emit vapors or gases in a well-ventilated area.
- Keep your hands away from your face while you are working on any activity.

Safety Symbols, continued

Electrical Safety

- Do not use equipment with frayed electrical cords or loose plugs.
- Do not use electrical equipment near water or when clothing or hands are wet.
- Hold the plug housing when you plug in or unplug equipment. Do not pull on the cord.
- Use only GFI-protected electrical receptacles.

Heating and Fire Safety

- Be aware of any source of flames, sparks, or heat (such as flames, heating coils, or hot plates) before working with any flammable substances.
- Know the location of the lab's fire extinguisher and fire-safety blankets.
- Know your school's fire-evacuation routes.
- If your clothing catches on fire, walk to the lab shower to put out the fire. Do not run.
- Never leave a hot plate unattended while it is turned on or while it is cooling.
- Use tongs or appropriately insulated holders when handling heated objects.
- Allow all equipment to cool before storing it.

Plant and Animal Safety

- Do not eat any part of a plant.
- Do not pick any wild plant unless your teacher instructs you to do so.
- Handle animals only as your teacher directs.
- Treat animals carefully and respectfully.
- Wash your hands thoroughly with soap and water after handling any plant or animal.

Cleanup

- Clean all work surfaces and protective equipment as directed by your teacher.
- Dispose of hazardous materials or sharp objects only as directed by your teacher.
- Wash your hands thoroughly with soap and water before you leave the lab or after any activity.

Student Safety Quiz

Circle the letter of the BEST answer.

1. Before starting an investigation or lab procedure, you should
   A. try an experiment of your own
   B. open all containers and packages
   C. read all directions and make sure you understand them
   D. handle all the equipment to become familiar with it

2. At the end of any activity you should
   A. wash your hands thoroughly with soap and water before leaving the lab
   B. cover your face with your hands
   C. put on your safety goggles
   D. leave hot plates switched on

3. If you get hurt or injured in any way, you should
   A. tell your teacher immediately
   B. find bandages or a first aid kit
   C. go to your principal's office
   D. get help after you finish the lab

4. If your glassware is chipped or broken, you should
   A. use it only for solid materials
   B. give it to your teacher for recycling or disposal
   C. put it back into the storage cabinet
   D. increase the damage so that it is obvious

5. If you have unused chemicals after finishing a procedure, you should
   A. pour them down a sink or drain
   B. mix them all together in a bucket
   C. put them back into their original containers
   D. dispose of them as directed by your teacher

6. If electrical equipment has a frayed cord, you should
   A. unplug the equipment by pulling the cord
   B. let the cord hang over the side of a counter or table
   C. tell your teacher about the problem immediately
   D. wrap tape around the cord to repair it

7. If you need to determine the odor of a chemical or a solution, you should
   A. use your hand to bring fumes from the container to your nose
   B. bring the container under your nose and inhale deeply
   C. tell your teacher immediately
   D. use odor-sensing equipment

8. When working with materials that might fly into the air and hurt someone's eye, you should wear
   A. goggles
   B. an apron
   C. gloves
   D. a hat

9. Before doing experiments involving a heat source, you should know the location of the
   A. door
   B. window
   C. fire extinguisher
   D. overhead lights

10. If you get chemicals in your eye you should
    A. wash your hands immediately
    B. put the lid back on the chemical container
    C. wait to see if your eye becomes irritated
    D. use the eyewash station right away, for a minimum of 15 minutes

Go online to view the Lab Safety Handbook for additional information.

The Flow of Energy in Systems

How does energy flow and cause water to cycle?

Flash floods can occur suddenly after a heavy rainfall. Flash floods release a lot of energy.

You Solve It How Can You Use the Sun's Energy?

Design a way to use the sun's energy to cook an egg and to heat water for people who are camping in the wilderness.

Go online and complete the You Solve It to explore ways to solve a real-world problem.

Explore Energy Flow in the Earth System

This rocky coastline is along Big Sur, California.

A. Look at the photo. On a separate sheet of paper, write down as many different questions as you can about the photo.

B. Discuss With your class or a partner, share your questions. Record any additional questions generated in your discussion. From the list choose the most important questions that are related to possible ways that energy could interact with different parts of the Earth system — atmosphere, geosphere, biosphere, and hydrosphere. Write them below.

C. What possible energy transformations or transfers will you research?

D. Use the information on this page, along with your research, to explore how surface materials interact with other surrounding materials.

Discuss the next steps for your Unit Project with your teacher and go online to download the Unit Project Worksheet.

Language Development

Use the lessons in this unit to complete the network and expand your understanding of these key concepts.

Similar term
Phrase
Cognate
Example
Definition

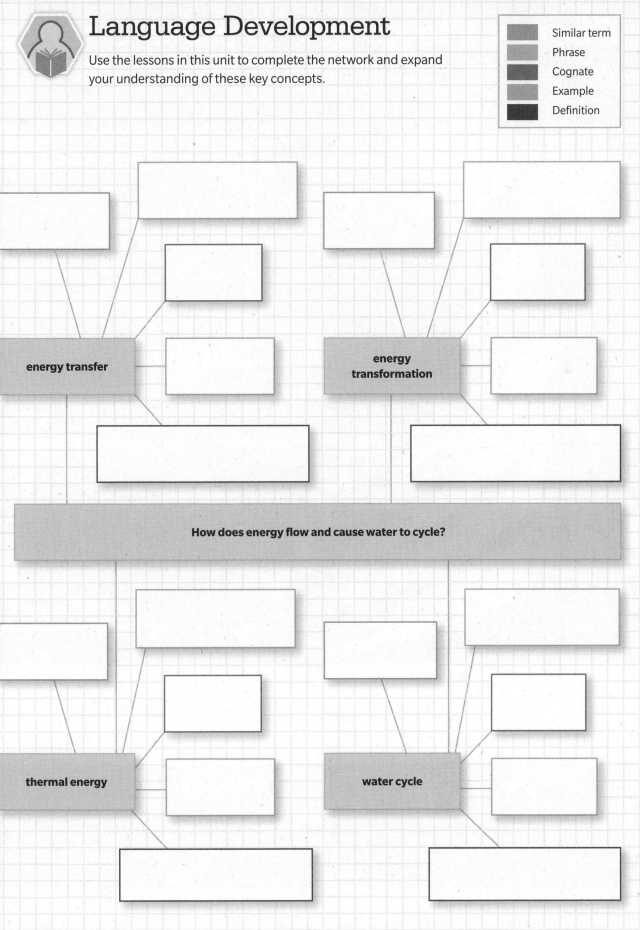

energy transfer

energy transformation

How does energy flow and cause water to cycle?

thermal energy

water cycle

Energy Flows and Causes Change

China's Three Gorges Dam hydroelectric power station transforms the energy of water into electrical energy.

Explore First

Moving Boxes Place three boxes of the same size on a table. In each box place a different size weight. Slide each box across the table. What do you notice about the energy that is required to move each box?

Go online to view the digital version of the Hands-On Lab for this lesson and to download additional lab resources.

CAN YOU EXPLAIN IT?

How can energy from the motion of the crank on a hand-powered flashlight produce light?

Hand-powered flashlights are useful tools in an emergency. They do not need replaceable batteries or other sources of electric power. Instead, the user turns a crank on the side of the flashlight. This causes the light bulb in the flashlight to light up.

1. How would you define the flashlight as a system? What are its inputs and outputs? What are the parts of the system?

2. The crank has the energy of motion when it is turned. What other types of energy might the flashlight have when the light bulb is on?

 EVIDENCE NOTEBOOK As you explore the lesson, gather evidence to help explain how turning the crank of a hand-powered flashlight produces light.

Identifying Different Forms of Energy

Energy is the ability to cause change. Processes and technologies that require energy are all around you. The movement of a clock's hands, the light from light fixtures, and the sounds made by electronic devices are all results of changes in energy. Understanding energy is important for making accurate weather forecasts. Weather prediction models account for energy transfers between the sun, our atmosphere, and oceans. This helps us understand when and where storms can develop.

Explore Online

You can observe many types of energy in a tornado.

3. **Discuss** What types of energy can you identify in the photo of the tornado?

The Energy of Matter in Motion: Kinetic Energy

A bowling ball rolling down a lane toward the pins is an example of a system that has energy. Evidence of this is the force that would be required to stop the rolling ball. A force was also used to send it rolling toward the pins. The energy that an object has due to its motion is called *kinetic energy*. All moving objects have kinetic energy. A bowling ball traveling down a lane, a skateboarder rolling down a ramp, and water rushing down a river are all systems that have kinetic energy.

Energy applied by the bowler started this ball moving.

Kinetic Energy and Mass

A bowling ball has a much greater mass than the tiny ball used in a pinball machine. Think about what would happen if you rolled these balls down the same bowling lane at the same speed.

4. What evidence could you use to compare the energy of the two balls? Which ball do you think has more energy? Write your answer in the table.

Type of Ball	Mass of Ball	Both balls are rolling at 2 m/s.	Kinetic Energy
Bowling Ball	6 kg		
Pinball	0.08 kg		

Kinetic energy is directly proportional to the mass of an object. In the example above, the bowling ball has more kinetic energy than the pinball. They are traveling at the same speed, but the bowling ball has more mass. The bowling ball has more kinetic energy because more energy was put into the system.

Kinetic Energy and Speed

Two balls with different masses moving at the same speed have different amounts of kinetic energy. Now think about how different speeds might affect kinetic energy.

5. Two bowlers each roll a 6 kg bowling ball down a lane. One ball rolls very fast. The other rolls slowly. Predict what will happen when each ball reaches the pins. What does your prediction tell you about how much energy each ball has? Write your prediction in the table.

Type of Ball	Mass of Ball	The balls are moving at different speeds.	Kinetic Energy
Bowling Ball	6 kg		
Bowling Ball	6 kg		

Kinetic energy is also proportional to the square of the object's velocity. A ball traveling at a fast speed has more kinetic energy than a ball of the same mass traveling at a slow speed. It would require more force to stop the fast ball than it would to stop the slow ball.

Stored Energy: Potential Energy

A ball at rest at the top of a hill does not have kinetic energy. As it rolls down the hill, it gains kinetic energy. Where does the kinetic energy gained by the ball come from? When the ball is at rest at the top of the hill, its position gives it the potential to begin rolling and gain kinetic energy. The energy stored in an object due to its position or condition is called *potential energy*. For example, increasing the height of the ball on the hill will increase its potential energy.

6. Think about how the ball's energy changes at different points on the hill.

   At the top of the hill, the ball's potential energy is at its ~~maximum~~ / minimum .
   As the ball rolls downhill, its kinetic energy increases / ~~decreases~~ and its potential energy ~~increases~~ / decreases . At the bottom of the hill, the ball's potential energy is at its ~~maximum~~ / minimum and its kinetic energy is at its maximum / ~~minimum~~ .

The ball speeds up as it rolls downhill. As the ball goes downhill, it gains kinetic energy and loses potential energy. The ball slows down as it rolls uphill. As the ball goes uphill, it loses kinetic energy and gains potential energy. The total energy does not change. Like matter, energy cannot be created or destroyed. That means that the total amount of energy in a system does not change unless energy is added to it or removed from it. This is known as the *law of conservation of energy*.

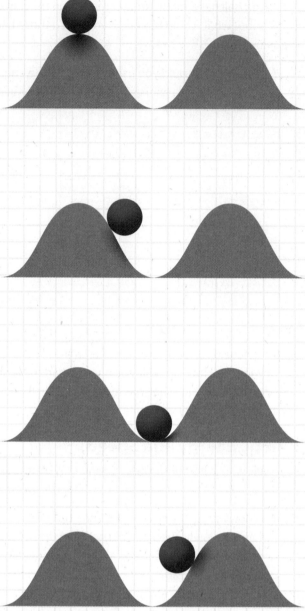

As the ball rolls downhill, its potential energy decreases. As the ball rolls up the next hill, its potential energy increases again.

Changes in Gravitational Potential Energy

Just as a ball on a hill will naturally roll downward because of gravity, the water at the top of a waterfall will flow downward. A pendulum released from the top of its arc will swing downward. Before they move downward, the ball, the water, and the pendulum have potential energy because of their positions.

The potential energy of an object due to its height, or its position relative to Earth's surface, is called *gravitational potential energy*. The higher an object is, the greater its gravitational potential energy.

For example, water a little bit upstream has more gravitational potential energy than it does at the top of the waterfall.

7. Rain drops move from clouds where they have _more / less_ gravitational potential energy to Earth's surface, where they have _more / less_ potential energy.

Imagine holding a ball in the air. If you let go, the ball will fall to the ground. It falls due to the pull of Earth's gravity. All objects tend to move from places where they have higher gravitational potential energy to places where they have lower gravitational potential energy. This means that balls do not roll uphill on their own. Pendulums do not spontaneously swing upward. Water does not flow up a waterfall on its own. However, you can make objects move upward by adding energy to them.

8. Where does the water in the photo have the least gravitational potential energy?

As water at the top of the waterfall flows downward, its potential energy decreases.

Forms of Energy

All energy is either potential energy or kinetic energy. Potential energy is due to an object's position or condition. Kinetic energy results from an object's motion. Each type of energy comes in different forms. Thermal energy, sound energy, electromagnetic energy, and electrical energy are forms of kinetic energy. Chemical energy, nuclear energy, gravitational potential energy, and elastic potential energy are forms of potential energy. All forms of energy are expressed in units of joules (J).

Mechanical Energy

Mechanical energy describes an object's ability to move—or do work on—other objects. It is the sum of the potential energy and kinetic energy of an object or a system. For example, a person swinging a hammer is providing kinetic energy to the hammer. The hammer does work on a nail. An object's mechanical energy can be all potential energy. It can be all kinetic energy. It can also be a combination of the two.

A hammer provides mechanical energy to do work on a nail.

Other Forms of Energy

You use many forms of energy every day. In fact, you are using several forms of energy as you explore this lesson. Electrical energy is a flow of negatively charged particles that generates the electric current that powers computers and lights. Chemical energy is the form of energy involved in chemical reactions. The battery on your cell phone uses chemical energy. Nuclear energy powers the sun. The sun gives off light energy that reaches Earth.

More than one form of energy can exist in a system at the same time. For example, fireworks explode because a huge amount of chemical potential energy is released. This energy becomes sound, light, and thermal energy.

The sun is the driving force behind many processes in Earth's systems. For example, energy from the sun causes the evaporation of water.

Thermal energy is the kinetic energy of the particles that make up matter. As its thermal energy increases, the glacier will melt at a faster rate and may retreat.

Sound energy is kinetic energy caused by the vibrations of the particles that make up matter. As the particles in the air vibrate, they transfer the sound energy to other particles. Your ears pick up the vibrations of particles in the air, which you hear as sound.

EVIDENCE NOTEBOOK

9. Think about the hand-cranked flashlight. What kinds of energy are involved in the operation of the flashlight? Record your evidence.

Analyze Applications of Mechanical Energy

Throughout history, people have designed machines that made the seemingly impossible possible. Many of these tools do work to increase the potential energy of an object or system. A simple lever can be used to lift a heavy boulder. Lifting it increases its potential energy. The lever can move the huge rock because the person using the lever adds kinetic energy by pushing the lever.

A towering 25-meter stone pillar called an obelisk stands in the center of St. Peter's Square in Rome. The 320,000-kilogram obelisk was put in place in 1586. The diagram shows how winches, shown as circles, were used. Some 900 workers and 75 horses pushed on levers to turn the winches, winding rope around their barrels. The ropes pulled on the obelisk to lift it into the place where it stands today.

10. Objects tend to come to rest at a position of lowest potential energy. Think of a machine or system that works against this tendency. Describe how kinetic energy is needed to increase the system's potential energy.

_____

_____

_____

_____

_____

_____

11. How might your machine or system be improved? What constraints might be involved in its design?

_____

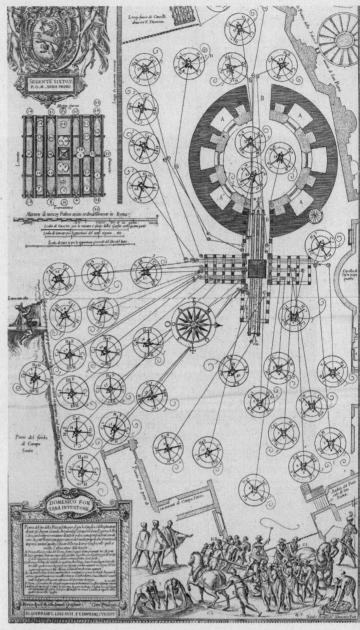

The Vatican Obelisk was first built by the Egyptians 3,200 years ago. This illustration shows how the obelisk was later installed in its current location in St. Peter's Square in Rome.

_____

_____

_____

_____

_____

_____

_____

Observing Energy Transfer

All forms of energy fall into two main categories—potential energy and kinetic energy. The position or condition of an object determines its potential energy. The speed and mass of an object determine its kinetic energy. A heavier object has greater kinetic energy than a lighter object moving at the same speed. And an object moving more quickly has more kinetic energy than a slower object with the same mass.

The bowling ball has kinetic energy because it is moving. As the ball hits the pins, it slows.

The bowling ball has kinetic energy as it moves toward the pins. The pins scatter in different directions when the ball hits them.

12. What happens to the kinetic energy of the bowling ball when the ball hits the pins?

13. Predict what will happen if the ball rolls straight into an object with a greater mass than a bowling pin.

Hands-On Lab
Investigate the Transfer of Energy

You will roll balls with different masses down a ramp at different heights. You will record how these factors affect the distance a cup moves when the balls hit it.

MATERIALS
- balance
- balls, of different masses
- books
- cardboard panel or plastic racecar track
- cup, plastic, with a section of the side cut out
- masking tape
- meterstick

Procedure and Analysis

STEP 1 Stack the books until they are about 20 cm high. Place one end of the cardboard panel or plastic racecar track on the books to make a ramp. Use masking tape to mark a starting point at the top of the ramp. Use a second piece of masking tape to mark a position near the bottom of the ramp where the target cup will be placed.

STEP 2 Use the balance to find the mass of Ball 1. Record the mass in the table below.

Ball	Mass	Distance moved: low ramp	Distance moved: high ramp
1			
2			
3			

STEP 3 Place the target cup with its cut side down on the masking tape. The open top of the cup should face the ramp so it can catch the ball. Release Ball 1 from the starting point at the top of the ramp. Measure the distance the cup moves after it catches the ball. Record your data in the table.

STEP 4 Repeat Steps 2 and 3 with other balls that have different masses.

STEP 5 Add books to the stack to increase the slope of the ramp. Repeat Steps 3 and 4.

STEP 6 How did the distance the cup moved change as the mass of the ball changed? How did the distance change as the height of the ramp changed?

STEP 7 **Language SmArts** On a separate sheet of paper, use the results of the activity to construct a statement about how mass and speed affect the transfer of kinetic energy. How can this investigation serve as a model for collisions in the real world?

Energy Transfer in Collisions

Objects that are not moving need energy to set them in motion. They carry that energy with them as they move. They can pass this kinetic energy to other objects when they collide. The passing of energy from one object to another is known as **energy transfer.** Because energy cannot be created or destroyed, you can model energy flowing through a system as inputs and outputs. Think about the bowling ball. It received an input of energy from the bowler. The ball carried that energy as it rolled down the lane. When the ball collided with a pin, it transferred energy to the pin. Energy is transferred from the object with more kinetic energy to the one with less kinetic energy. The pin moves because energy was transferred to it.

Energy is transferred from the bowler's hand to the bowling ball. Then it is transferred from the bowling ball to the pin.

Energy transfers in other types of collisions can also be modeled. For example, energy is transferred within the system when a swinging pendulum hits a pendulum that is not moving. Transferring kinetic energy to an object can move it to a position with higher potential energy.

Energy Transfer between Objects of the Same Size and Mass

14. Two pendulums are set to collide. Identify where the swinging pendulum has the greatest potential energy and where it has the greatest kinetic energy. Draw an arrow in the second photo to show the transfer of energy between the pendulums during the collision.

• greatest potential energy	• greatest kinetic energy

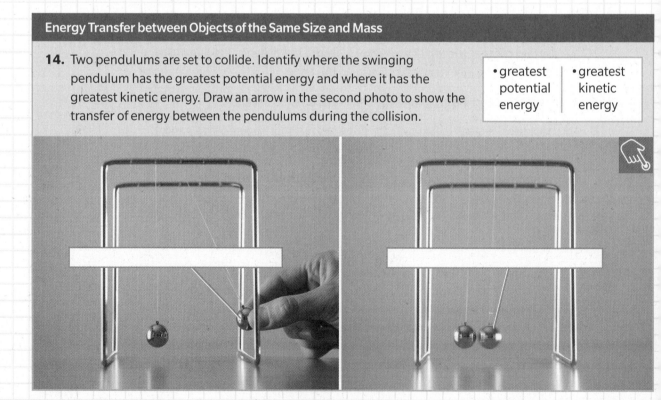

Energy Transfer in a Newton's Cradle

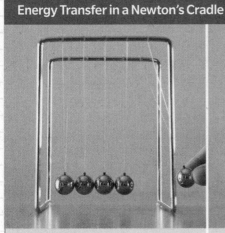  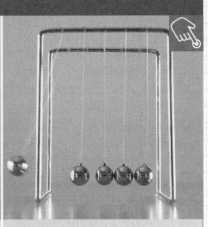

When the pendulum is pulled back, it has its greatest amount of potential energy.

Upon collision, the kinetic energy is transferred from one pendulum to the next.

The transfer of kinetic energy causes the last pendulum to move and gain potential energy.

In the earlier pendulum collision, the kinetic energy from the moving pendulum is transferred to the motionless one. The transfer of kinetic energy causes the stationary pendulum to move to a position of greater potential energy than it had at its starting point. That system only had two pendulums. Explore what happens when multiple objects are involved in a transfer of energy within a system. These photos show a Newton's cradle, a series of identical pendulums hanging side by side.

15. Draw Create a diagram showing the transfer of energy between two objects. You can base your diagram on a Newton's cradle .

Energy in Machines

Transfers of kinetic energy are used in devices and processes that reduce human effort. Energy transfer can also be used to do things that the human body alone would not be able to do.

The downward flow of water in a river is the result of the pull of gravity. As water moves downhill, its potential energy transforms into kinetic energy Kinetic energy can also be used to do other work, as in a water wheel. A water wheel can be used to turn a gristmill, which uses the energy to grind grains for flour.

Energy from flowing water is transferred to the water wheel, causing it to turn.

Energy Transfer in the Earth System

Energy transfers in the Earth system drive many processes, including weathering and erosion. For example, in rivers, the kinetic energy of flowing water can be transferred to sediment on the river bottom. If enough energy is transferred, rocks move along the river bottom or move downstream in the water. The moving rocks may collide with other rocks. Kinetic energy can be transferred during these collisions. The collisions can also cause the rocks to break down and become smoother.

Water transfers kinetic energy to the boulders in this river.

EVIDENCE NOTEBOOK

16. Describe the transfer of kinetic energy that occurs between a person and the crank of a hand-cranked flashlight. Record your evidence.

Analyze Meteoroid Deflection

Stony or metallic space objects, known as *meteoroids,* often enter Earth's atmosphere. Most are small. They burn up before they reach Earth's surface. Rarely, larger chunks traveling at extremely high speeds hit Earth's surface. Because of their high speeds, the objects have a large amount of kinetic energy. Such an impact can have disastrous results.

In 1908, a 91-million-kilogram space rock entered Earth's atmosphere above Tunguska, Siberia. The rock exploded in the sky, producing a huge fireball that destroyed 2,000 square kilometers of forest. A similar blast happened over another site in Russia in 2013, injuring 1,500 people and damaging thousands of buildings.

This photo shows a portion of the forest destroyed in the aftermath of the Tunguska event.

17. One idea for avoiding a catastrophic collision of space debris with Earth is the use of missile-like projectiles to knock the object off course, or deflect it. How can scientists be sure to create an impact with enough kinetic energy to change a meteoroid's course? What factors should they consider?

_____

_____

_____

_____

_____

_____

Modeling Energy Transformations

As you observed with the Newton's cradle, kinetic energy is transferred between objects when one object collides with another. However, if you continued to watch the pendulums, you would observe that they gradually swing lower and lower until they eventually come to a stop.

18. Why do you think the Newton's cradle stops swinging? What does this imply about the energy in the system of pendulums?

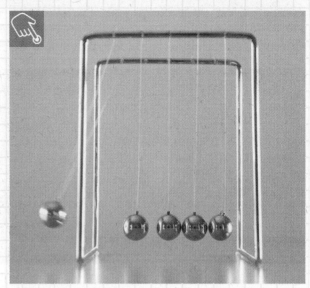

As the action of the Newton's cradle progresses over time, the pendulums gradually slow to a stop.

Transformations: Changes in the Form of Energy

You can see the transfer of kinetic energy when one pendulum hits another. Energy also seems to be lost gradually from the system as the pendulums lose speed and height with each swing. The law of conservation of energy says that energy cannot be created or destroyed, so the "lost" energy must transfer somewhere else or be changed in some way.

19. Think about collisions and what you know about different forms of energy. What other forms of energy might result from collisions in a Newton's cradle?

When the pendulums collide, they make a sound. This sound is evidence that some of the energy transferred during the collision changes form. Some of the energy becomes sound energy. The collisions also increase the kinetic energy of the particles that make up the pendulums. This increases the thermal energy of the system. The process of one form of energy changing to another form is known as **energy transformation.** It differs from simple energy transfer in which energy moves from one object to another, or from one place to another while staying in the same form.

Everyday Uses of Energy Transformations

The process of energy transformation happens all the time and everywhere. In fact, all of the electronic technologies you use every day need energy transformations to work. Refrigerators, microwave ovens, lights, batteries, and cars all rely on energy transformations. These devices make use of the fact that any form of energy can transform into any other form of energy. For example, a personal music player transforms electrical energy to sound energy and thermal energy.

The chemical energy stored in fireworks is transformed into electromagnetic, sound, and thermal energy.

Electrical energy is transformed into electromagnetic energy and sound energy in a television or computer monitor.

Batteries power electronic devices by transforming chemical energy into electrical energy.

People can also generate electrical energy. Wind-up radios work by converting kinetic energy from a person to electrical energy.

Alternative Energy and Energy Transformations

Today, many people are looking for energy sources other than fossil fuels. Many alternative energy sources transform mechanical energy into electrical energy. In hydroelectric dams, the kinetic energy of flowing water is transferred to a generator that transforms that energy into electrical energy. Windmills work in a similar way and use the kinetic energy of wind to generate electrical energy. Tidal energy provides power by converting the kinetic energy of moving ocean water into electrical energy. Solar panels do not use kinetic energy. Instead, they transform light energy from the sun directly into electrical energy.

 EVIDENCE NOTEBOOK

20. What energy transformations occur in the hand-cranked flashlight? Record your evidence.

Energy Loss in a System

Think about a Newton's cradle again. During the collisions, some energy is transferred between the pendulums as mechanical energy. Some energy is also transformed into sound and thermal energy. What happens to the energy that is converted into sound and thermal energy?

21. Draw Reconsider the diagram of energy transfer within the Newton's cradle system you created earlier in this lesson. How would you revise your model to account for the transformations of energy that also occur during the collisions between the pendulums? Where are the additional forms of energy transferred?

The energy from the pendulum collisions that is transformed into sound energy is carried through vibrations of the molecules in the air around the pendulums. The energy that is transformed into thermal energy is also transferred to the surrounding air. With each collision, this energy is transferred away from the Newton's cradle.

Because energy cannot be created or destroyed, transfers of energy away from a system to its surroundings result in an overall loss of energy from the system. The loss of energy from a system may seem minor, but over time it adds up. The motion of the pendulums in a Newton's cradle decreases as the system loses energy. Eventually, the cradle comes to a complete stop. An input of kinetic energy is needed to start the cradle swinging again.

Do the Math | Energy Efficiency The ratio of useful energy output to the overall energy input in a system is known as *efficiency*. Incandescent light bulbs are not efficient. They transform a large portion of electrical energy into thermal energy instead of light. To save energy, these bulbs have been replaced with compact fluorescent lamps (CFLs) and light-emitting diodes (LEDs). CFLs and LEDs use less electrical energy to produce the same amount of light.

The flow of energy through a system can be expressed in watts (W). One watt is equal to the flow of one joule of energy for one second. This table shows data for three bulbs that produce the same amount of light. Electrical energy is often measured in kilowatt-hours (kW•h), or the amount of energy used in one hour at the rate of 1,000 W (J/s).

Energy Used by Light Bulbs		
Bulb type	Watts (J/s)	Energy used over 2,000 hours (kW•h)
Incandescent	60	120
CFL	14	28
LED	10	20

22. Suppose the price of electricity is 12.75 cents per kW•h. What is the difference in cost in dollars between the use of an incandescent bulb for 2,000 hours and an LED bulb for the same amount of time?

23. How much more energy (in J) does an incandescent bulb use than a CFL in one minute?

Describe Efficient Energy Use

Laptops and other electronic devices become warm when they are in use. Some of the chemical energy from the battery is transformed into thermal energy instead of electrical energy. Much of the electrical energy produced by the battery becomes thermal energy as it flows through the computer parts. The electrical energy is useful, but the thermal energy is not. The battery loses chemical energy in both useful and non-useful transformations as it is used.

A laptop battery produces thermal energy.

24. Hand-cranked flashlights transform mechanical energy into other forms of energy. Which energy transformations are useful, and which are not? Explain why most hand-cranked flashlights are made with LEDs.

_____

_____

_____

_____

Continue Your Exploration

Name: _____   Date: _____

Check out the path below or go online to choose one of the other paths shown.

Moving Water Uphill

- **Hydroelectric Power**
- **Hands-On Labs** 🖐
- **Propose Your Own Path**

Go online to choose one of these other paths.

A water wheel uses kinetic energy from flowing water to power machinery. In this use, mechanical energy supplied by moving water is used to power another process. Another type of water wheel, called a *noria*, is not used to supply mechanical energy for other processes. A noria's only purpose is to raise water to a higher location.

A noria is similar to other water wheels, except that it has open containers along the outer rim of its wheel. The containers fill with water when they are lowered into a body of flowing water, such as a river, as the wheel turns. As the wheel continues to turn, the containers of water are lifted. During this upward movement, the containers overturn and empty the water into a higher trough or aqueduct. The water can then be transported to another location for irrigation or use in towns and villages.

1. Kinetic energy from water flowing in the river is transferred to the noria, which lifts water from the river to the aqueduct. How does the gravitational potential energy of the water change as it approaches the top of the wheel?

   A. Its gravitational potential energy does not change.

   B. Its gravitational potential energy increases.

   C. Its gravitational potential energy decreases.

The norias of Hama, Syria, are the largest in the world. They were used for centuries to lift water from the Orontes River. Today, they are mostly unused.

Continue Your Exploration

As water reaches the top of the wheel, it pours into a collecting trough.

2. The norias of Hama are known for creaking loudly as they turn. Which statement about a noria is correct?

   A. Some kinetic energy of the noria is transformed into sound energy.

   B. Some kinetic energy of the noria is transformed into light energy.

   C. The kinetic energy of the noria does not change.

   D. The noria does not have any input or output of energy.

3. Paddle boats are boats that are propelled by a paddle wheel using similar mechanics as a water wheel. A water wheel is propelled by flowing water. A paddle boat can be operated using human power, a steam engine, or solar power. Describe the energy transfers and transformations that take place within the paddle wheel system.

4. **Collaborate** Water wheels can be good sources of renewable energy. Norias help people use water resources. Because these devices rely on running water to function, they are not always reliable. Discuss how the availability of flowing water affects the usefulness of a water wheel. Discuss how you might plan ahead to deal with changes in conditions, such as a drought.

Can You Explain It?

Name: _____ **Date:** _____

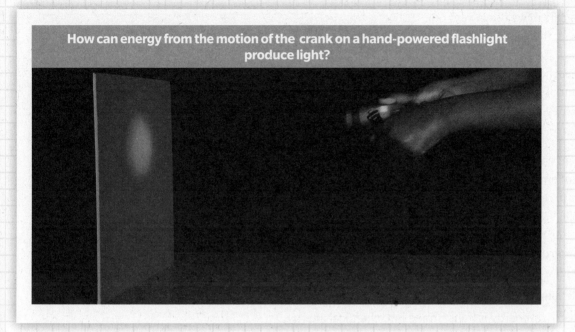

How can energy from the motion of the crank on a hand-powered flashlight produce light?

 EVIDENCE NOTEBOOK

Refer to the notes in your Evidence Notebook to help you construct an explanation for how the input of mechanical energy with the crank is able to produce an output of light.

1. State your claim. Make sure your claim fully explains the transfers and transformations of energy within the system.

2. Summarize the evidence you have gathered to support your claim and explain your reasoning.

Checkpoints

Answer the following questions to check your understanding of the lesson.

Use the photo of the roller coaster to answer Questions 3 and 4.

3. As the cars move downward on the loop, their kinetic energy *decreases / increases*. The cars have the greatest amount of potential energy when they are at the *bottom / top* of the loop.

4. A roller coaster car requires an input of energy from an electric motor to reach the top of the first hill. Which statement describes the transformation of energy involved in this process?

   A. Mechanical energy is transformed into electrical energy.

   B. Electrical energy is transformed into chemical energy.

   C. Electrical energy is transformed into mechanical energy.

   D. No energy transformation occurs.

Use the table to answer Question 5.

5. Each of the balls in the table collided with a stationary object of the same mass. Which statements about the transfer of kinetic energy are correct? Choose all that apply.

   A. Ball A and Ball B transfer the same amount of energy.

   B. Ball B transfers more energy than Ball A.

   C. Ball B and Ball C transfer the same amount of energy.

   D. Ball C transfers more energy than Ball B.

Ball	Mass (g)	Velocity (m/s)
Ball A	45	30
Ball B	45	40
Ball C	60	40

---

6. When a meteoroid strikes Earth, mechanical energy is transformed into which of these forms of energy? Choose all that apply.

   A. sound energy

   B. thermal energy

   C. electrical energy

   D. chemical energy

Interactive Review

Complete this section to review the main concepts of the lesson.

Kinetic energy is the energy of an object due to its speed and mass. Potential energy is the energy of an object due to its position or condition.

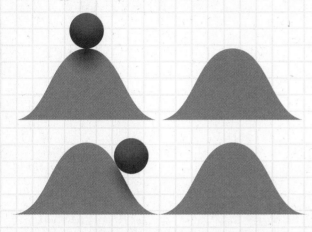

A. Describe how the speed and mass of an object affect the amount of kinetic energy of the object.

Changes in kinetic energy involve a transfer of energy to or from an object.

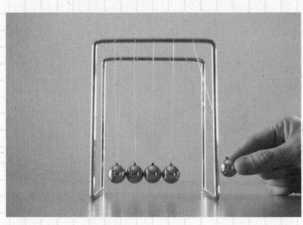

B. Describe the transfer of energy between the pendulums in a Newton's cradle.

A change in energy from one form to another is known as an energy transformation. Any form of energy can transform into any other form of energy.

C. Explain how evidence of energy transformations in fireworks supports the law of conservation of energy.

Heat Is a Flow of Energy

Even when the temperature outside is very low, an insulated coat can keep you warm.

Explore First

Comparing Temperatures Fill a glass beaker and a paper cup each with warm or hot water that is at the same temperature. Touch the outside of each container. What do you observe?

Go online to view the digital version of the Hands-On Lab for this lesson and to download additional lab resources.

CAN YOU EXPLAIN IT?

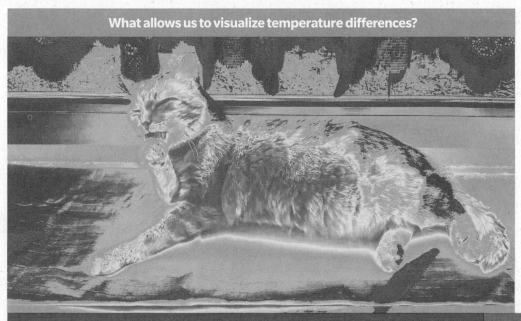

What allows us to visualize temperature differences?

Most photographs use visible light to make an image. These images are similar to what we see with our eyes. Infrared photography, though, can generate an image that shows temperature differences. In this image, different colors indicate different temperatures.

Explore Online

1. What does it mean for objects to be at different temperatures? What is different about them physically?

2. Why do you think different temperatures appear as different colors on an infrared image?

EVIDENCE NOTEBOOK As you explore the lesson, gather evidence to help explain how temperature differences could be visualized.

Comparing Hot and Cold Objects

You come into contact with hot and cold objects every day. Objects that are hot, relative to their surroundings, do not stay that way. They will eventually cool. For example, hot soup begins to cool as soon as it is taken off the stove burner. Objects that are cold, relative to their surroundings, will warm. An ice cube starts to warm and melt as soon as it leaves the freezer.

3. Ice cubes melt if you leave them out on a warm day. Describe this process in terms of energy and temperature.

4. Imagine you are holding an ice cube. Draw a diagram that shows how your hand, the ice cube, and the air around your hand and the ice cube are warming or cooling. Use arrows to show how energy is being transferred from one object or substance to another.

As the ice cubes warm, their particles have more kinetic energy.

The Direction of Energy Transfer

If a hot pan is placed on a cool counter, the pan will spontaneously warm both the countertop and the surrounding air. As the pan warms the countertop and air, the pan cools. This process continues until the pan, the air, and the countertop are all the same temperature. In the same way, if a cold pack is placed on your forehead, your forehead will cool and the cold pack will warm until they are the same temperature. When objects are at different temperatures, energy is transferred from the warmer object to the cooler object. This energy transfer can be modeled by using arrows to show how energy is flowing from warmer objects to cooler objects.

5. When two objects at different temperatures are in contact, thermal energy flows from the cooler / warmer object into the cooler / warmer object until the temperatures increase / are the same in both objects.

Hot and Cold

When you touch an object and it feels warm, it is because energy is being transferred from that object to you. When an object feels cold, energy is being transferred from you to the object. Energy flows from warmer objects to cooler objects. So, an object will usually feel warm to the touch if it is at a higher temperature than your hand. And if an object is at a lower temperature than your hand, it usually feels cool to the touch.

6. If you hold a glass of cold water, your hand will become cold. Describe how energy flows in this situation.

A hot pan on a countertop will transfer energy to the countertop and to the air around it until the pan, the countertop, and the air are all the same temperature.

Energy is transferred from the hot liquid to the spoon and then from the hot spoon to your hand. This energy transfer causes the spoon to feel warm relative to your hand.

Analyze the Loss of Thermal Energy

7. Recall the photo of the melting ice cubes. If you put the water from the melted ice cubes back into the freezer, it will become solid again. Describe the transfer of thermal energy as the ice cubes melt and then as they become solid again. In both situations, describe which substances are gaining and losing energy.

_____

_____

_____

_____

Relating Temperature and Thermal Energy

Suppose you have two similar rocks in front of you. One rock has been sitting in the shade, and the other has been sitting in the sunlight. The two rocks look the same, but if you touch them, you will observe a difference. One rock will feel cold and the other rock will feel warm because the temperatures of the rocks are different. When you touch the rocks, you will know right away which one was in the sunlight.

These rock outcrops are in the Mojave Desert in California.

8. **Discuss** How will the temperature of a rock in the desert change throughout the day and night?

Temperature

Think back to the hot and cold rocks. What makes one rock hot and the other cold? Like all matter, the rocks are made up of particles that are too small to be seen. These particles are in constant motion. Like all objects in motion, these particles have energy. The energy associated with their motion is kinetic energy. The faster the particles move, the greater their kinetic energy is.

9. The rock sitting in the sunlight feels hotter because its particles are moving
   faster / slower than the particles in the rock that is sitting in the shade.

   Temperature is a measure of the average kinetic energy of all the particles in an object or substance. Temperature does not depend on the material or the type of particles in a substance.

Thermal Energy

Temperature is a measure of the average kinetic energy of an object. **Thermal energy** is the measurement of the total amount of kinetic energy of all the particles in an object or substance. Thermal energy is measured in joules (J). All matter has thermal energy. When an object is hot, its particles are moving faster and it has more thermal energy than it has when it is cold.

A quarter and a dime are made of the same materials. If the two coins have the same temperature, the quarter has more thermal energy than the dime. Although the average kinetic energy of their particles is the same, the quarter has many more particles than the dime, so the quarter has more total thermal energy.

quarter

dime

10. If you warmed the dime until it melted, the melted dime would have more / less thermal energy than the solid dime had. This is because the particles in the melted dime are moving faster / slower than the solid particles were. So the particles of the melted dime have more / less kinetic energy.

Consider a glass of ice water in which the water and ice are both close to the same temperature. The liquid water has more thermal energy than an equal mass of ice, even though they are at the same temperature. Liquid particles move much faster and have more energy than solid particles. Similarly, the particles in a gas have more energy than the particles in the liquid phase of the same substance.

Different kinds of matter are made up of different kinds of particles that do not interact with one another in the same way in each substance. Because of these differences, the amount of thermal energy in two different substances with equal mass can be different even if they have the same temperature.

11. If two objects have the same temperature, will they always have the same thermal energies? Record your evidence.

Hands-On Lab
Compare Thermal Energy in Objects

You will plan an investigation to determine what properties affect the amount of thermal energy in an object.

Procedure

You will need to use a hot water bath for this investigation. Your teacher will guide you in making one.

As you develop your plan, consider these questions:

- How can you indirectly determine the thermal energy of the objects? (Hint: Think about how a hot object would affect water if placed in the water.)
- What data should you measure and record?
- Which objects will you test to provide data to answer your questions?

STEP 1 Plan and write your procedure to determine the properties that affect the amount of thermal energy an object. Your procedure should describe how to test the amount of thermal energy that four different objects have.

MATERIALS
- bowl, wide, flat bottom
- cups, small, plastic foam (5)
- graduated cylinder, 25 mL
- hot plate
- ice water
- thermometers, non-mercury (6)
- tongs
- washers, aluminum, 10 g
- washers, aluminum, 20 g
- water
- weight, brass, 20 g
- weight, rubber, 10 g

STEP 2 Get your teacher's approval before you begin your investigation. Make any changes to your procedure requested by your teacher.

STEP 3 Perform your investigation, following the steps you have written. Record your observations on a separate sheet of paper.

STEP 4 Rank the objects by the amount of thermal energy they seemed to contain.

1. _____

2. _____

3. _____

4. _____

STEP 5 Which factors seem to affect the amount of thermal energy an object has?
Select all that apply.

A. mass

B. shape

C. color

D. material

STEP 6 **Language SmArts** Trade procedures with another group and follow
the steps that they used. Did you get the same results? Why or why not?

STEP 7 If the water in two different lakes is at the same temperature, can the lakes have
different amounts of thermal energy? Explain your answer.

Factors Affecting the Thermal Energy in an Object

Every object has thermal energy because every object's particles are moving. In the
Hands-On Lab, when you placed a hot object in cold water, the temperature of the water
increased. The change in water temperature was not the same for all of the objects.
The object with the larger mass had more energy than the smaller object of the same
material at the same temperature. Because it had more energy, the larger object warmed
the water to a higher temperature after a certain amount of time.

The brass and aluminum objects that had the same mass warmed the water by
different amounts, so this is evidence that the thermal energy of an object also depends
on the material it is made of. Different materials of the same size and same temperature
can have different amounts of thermal energy.

 EVIDENCE NOTEBOOK

12. The infrared photograph indicates that the surfaces and air near the cat
are warmer than the surfaces and air farther away. What factors might
cause these temperature differences? Record your evidence.

Do the Math

Compare Objects' Thermal Energies

All matter has some amount of thermal energy—even the coldest object you have ever felt. But the actual amount of thermal energy varies among objects of different temperatures and of different materials. The thermal energy in any object is related to its mass, composition, state, and temperature.

13. Look at the photos of the two rocks and the information in the caption. Think about how the rocks are different. Which rock has a greater amount of thermal energy? Explain your answer.

These two rocks are made of the same substance and are the same temperature, but have different masses. The rock on the right has significantly less mass than the rock on the left.

14. Place these objects in order by the amount of thermal energy they contain. Number the boxes so that they are ordered from least thermal energy (1) to greatest thermal energy (5). Assume that the iceberg and the lake have similar masses.

ice: __1__

iceberg: _____

boiling water: _____

water: _____

lake: _____

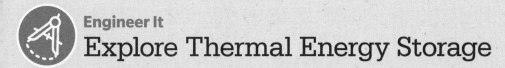

Engineer It

Explore Thermal Energy Storage

Energy from the sun can be captured in solar power plants and used by humans. At night and on some cloudy days, solar power plants do not generate any energy. At other times, solar power plants generate more electrical energy than people need. A thermal battery is one way to store the extra energy for use later. When the sun is shining, the system adds thermal energy to a solid, such as salt. As the thermal energy of the salt increases, it melts. The energy stored in the molten material is later used to warm other objects or produce an electric current.

This giant mirror focuses sunlight onto material in the box.

15. Some solar power plants use mirrors to focus sunlight on a central collector. The energy from sunlight causes water in the central collector to boil and produce steam. A generator uses the kinetic energy of the steam to produce electrical energy. How could a thermal battery help this type of power plant generate electrical energy 24 hours per day?

_____

_____

_____

_____

_____

_____

_____

_____

_____

_____

_____

Analyzing Heat

Suppose that you are standing outside on a sunny day. The skin on your arms feels very warm in the sunlight. Suddenly a cloud comes between you and the sun. A thermometer would show that the temperature of the air near you has not changed very much. Your skin feels much cooler, though. As the cloud moves away, you start to feel warmer.

A sunny place usually feels warmer than a shady place, even if a thermometer shows little to no temperature difference in the air.

16. Why might you feel warmer in a sunny place than in a shady place, even though the air temperature is the same?

Heat

Think about what happens when you boil water on the stove. The pot of water becomes warmer while it is over the stove. This is because thermal energy is being transferred to the water. Energy flows from the stove to the pot of water as heat. You may have heard *heat* used in other ways in everyday language, but in science, heat has a specific definition. **Heat** is the energy that is transferred between two objects that are at different temperatures.

When thermal energy is transferred to an object as heat, the average kinetic energy of the particles in the object will increase. And so, the temperature of the object will rise. Heat always flows from an object at a higher temperature to an object at a lower temperature. Heat will flow as long as there is a temperature difference. If no energy is added to the system, both objects will eventually have the same temperature.

It is sometimes helpful to know how much thermal energy is needed to change the temperature of a substance by a certain amount. For example, a materials scientist might want to know how much energy it would take to melt a metal sample. The amount of thermal energy needed to change the temperature of a substance depends on the identity of the substance, the mass of the sample, and the system surrounding the substance.

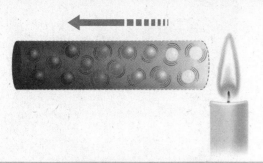

Conduction Thermal energy is transferred between particles through conduction. In this example, the candle is warming one end of the metal bar. The particles in the metal bar start to move faster as they gain more thermal energy. As the particles move faster, they bump into each other and transfer thermal energy through the metal rod.

Convection Thermal energy is transferred throughout liquids and gases through convection. In this example, the candle is heating the box. As air in the box warms, the air particles begin to move faster and the air becomes less dense. The colder, denser air sinks and pushes up the warmer air. This movement transfers thermal energy through liquids and gases.

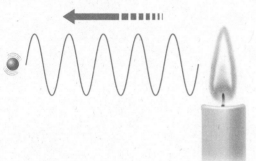

Radiation Radiation is the transfer of energy through electromagnetic waves. In this example, the candle produces infrared radiation. This radiation travels through empty space until it hits a particle. The particle then absorbs this radiation, and the radiation is converted into thermal energy. This process is how thermal energy is transferred through space.

Three Types of Thermal Energy Transfer

To remove a metal pan from a hot oven, you must use an insulated pad or glove. If you do not, energy will transfer quickly to your hand by conduction. The pan is much hotter than your skin, so its particles have a lot more thermal energy. When the particles of the metal bump into the particles of your skin, energy is transferred.

When the hot pan is on top of the stove, you can tell that it is hot by holding your hand above the pan. The moving air around the pan absorbs energy and carries it to your skin by convection. You can also absorb energy by holding your hand to the side of a stove's heating element. Energy is transferred through radiation to your skin.

Energy in the form of heat can be transferred by conduction, convection, and radiation. During all three types of energy transfer, the thermal energy of the warmer object decreases and the thermal energy of the cooler object increases. In all three types of energy transfer, energy is being transferred to a cooler object.

 EVIDENCE NOTEBOOK

17. Infrared photography produces images showing the temperature ranges of different objects. What type of energy transfer is necessary for infrared photography? Explain your answer.

18. Explain how each of the three types of energy transfer occurs in a solar oven while it cooks a bowl of soup.

Radiation carries energy from the sun. In a solar oven, this energy is directed at a single object to cook food.

19. Act With your group, plan a short skit to model one of the three methods of thermal energy transfer. Focus on making your performance convey information as accurately as possible. Record the plan for your skit and then perform it for the class.

Compare Thermal Conductivities

Different substances can absorb or transfer energy at different rates. For example, cooks often prefer a wooden spoon to a metal spoon for stirring a hot liquid. This is because a spoon made of wood absorbs energy slowly and will not get very hot. A metal spoon will absorb energy quickly and become too hot to hold. Thermal conductivity is a property of matter that refers to how quickly a material transfers and absorbs energy as heat.

20. Suppose you are designing a heat exchanger to remove energy from a motor as quickly as possible. Energy will be transferred from the motor to the heat exchanger. Then the energy will be transferred from the heat exchanger to the air. The table shows the thermal conductivities of a few substances as measured in W/m·K. The greater the thermal conductivity, the faster the rate of energy transfer. Which material would be the best choice?

Substance	Thermal conductivity (W/m·K)
Copper	385
Glass	0.8
Polystyrene	0.033
Steel	50

A. copper

B. glass

C. polystyrene

D. steel

Continue Your Exploration

Name: _____   Date: _____

Check out the path below or go online to choose one of the other paths shown.

Heat and Cooking

- **Heat and Computing**
- **Hands-On Labs** 🖐
- **Propose Your Own Path**

Go online to choose one of these other paths.

A good cook must understand temperature, thermal energy, and heat. The energy added to food during cooking causes chemical changes in the food. It is important to control the amount of energy absorbed by the food. Too much energy, and the food will be overcooked. Too little energy, and food will still be raw. It is also important to control the rate of energy transfer. If energy is added too quickly or too slowly, the food may have the wrong texture or it might cook unevenly.

1. How might using a pizza stone instead of a pan affect how the pizza cooks?

   A. The stone gets hotter than the rest of the oven, so the pizza cooks faster.

   B. The stone transfers energy slowly, so the crust cooks evenly.

   C. The stone absorbs energy, keeping the crust cooler than the pizza toppings.

2. Pizza restaurants often use large ovens lined with bricks. These ovens remain very hot, even though only a small fire is kept burning in the oven. Why might this be?

Pizzas can be cooked in an oven using a pizza stone, a pizza pan, or no pan at all. The pizza stone absorbs and releases energy more slowly than a pizza pan does.

Continue Your Exploration

If food is cooked too quickly, the outside can burn, while the inside of the food is still raw.

3. What might cause the food to not cook all the way through?

   A. Not enough energy reaches the center of the food.

   B. Energy flows into the food too quickly and is lost before the inside is cooked.

   C. The food conducts energy, so the energy passes through the food without cooking it.

   D. The energy cooks the outside of the food, and then the food begins to lose heat instead of cooking further.

4. If the oven is too hot, the bottom part of cookies on a metal tray can become hard and black. Why would the bottom of the cookies burn first?

5. **Collaborate** With a partner, research one or more recipes. Make a presentation that shows how the method of cooking described in the recipe or recipes affects the food.

Can You Explain It?

Name: **Date:**

What allows us to visualize temperature differences?

Explore Online

EVIDENCE NOTEBOOK

Refer to the notes in your Evidence Notebook to help you construct an explanation for how infrared photography can be used to visualize temperature differences.

1. State your claim. Make sure your claim fully explains how infrared photography can be used to visualize temperature differences.

2. Summarize the evidence you have gathered to support your claim and explain your reasoning.

Checkpoints

Answer the following questions to check your understanding of the lesson.

Use the photo to answer Question 3.

3. Energy flows through a system that consists of the stove, the pan, the boiling water, and the air around these objects. Which of the following statements describe a direction that energy is moving in this system? Select all that apply.

 A. the stove to the pan

 B. the pan to the water

 C. the water to the pan

 D. the pan to the stove

4. Suppose you had a glass that was partially filled with water. Which of the following statements describe ways that you could raise the thermal energy of the glass of water? Select all that apply.

 A. Remove water from the glass.

 B. Add water of the same temperature to the glass.

 C. Warm the glass of water using a microwave.

 D. Cool the glass of water using a refrigerator.

Use the photo and table to answer Questions 5–6.

5. On a sunny day, the sidewalk and the street are both warmer than the atmosphere because they have more heat / thermal energy due to energy transfer by conduction / radiation from the sun.

6. A student used a thermometer to measure the temperature at three places and recorded the data in a table. Which statements represent conclusions that you can support with these data? Select all that apply.

 A. The temperature of the sidewalk is the same as the temperature of the street.

 B. Energy has been transferred from the street to the air above the street.

 C. Energy has been transferred from the lawn to the street and sidewalk through conduction.

 D. The street surface has absorbed more radiant thermal energy than the sidewalk.

Location	Temperature
0.5 m above street	38 °C
0.5 m above sidewalk	33 °C
0.5 m above grass lawn	27 °C

Interactive Review

Complete this section to review the main concepts of the lesson.

Humans perceive objects as hot or cold due to temperature differences and the transfer of energy.

A. Recall a situation when you felt a hot or cold object. Discuss the temperature differences involved and the direction in which the energy was being transferred.

Thermal energy is the total kinetic energy of the particles that make up a substance. Temperature is a measure of the average kinetic energy of the particles that make up a substance.

B. Describe how an object's thermal energy will change and how the particles in the object will be affected when the object's temperature increases.

Heat is the energy transferred between two objects that are at different temperatures. Energy in the form of heat can be transferred by conduction, convection, or radiation.

C. Describe situations in which energy is transferred through conduction, convection, and radiation.

Using Thermal Energy Transfer in Systems

Used, or *spent*, nuclear fuel rods are stored at the bottom of a cooling pool at the nuclear power plant in Chinon, France.

Explore First

Observing a Thermal Energy Transfer Pour water into a beaker and add a few drops of food coloring. Warm the bottom of the jar. What do you observe about the movement of the food coloring and water in the jar?

Go online to view the digital version of the Hands-On Lab for this lesson and to download additional lab resources.

CAN YOU EXPLAIN IT?

Why are urban heat islands hotter than their surrounding regions?

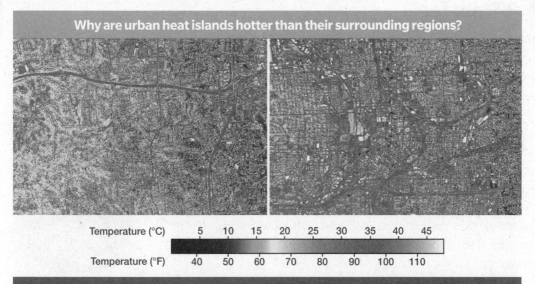

Temperature (°C) 5 10 15 20 25 30 35 40 45

Temperature (°F) 40 50 60 70 80 90 100 110

These satellite images of suburban (left) and urban (right) Atlanta, Georgia, show the differences in daytime temperatures in the region. The images show the two areas at the same time and on the same day.

Using a variety of tools ranging from thermometers to satellite images, scientists have collected data about the average temperatures in many places. The data show that urban areas are often significantly warmer than the rural places nearby. These warmer areas inside cities are called *urban heat islands*.

1. Think about how surfaces in cities differ from those in the surrounding areas. Why might a central city contain more thermal energy than a farm or forest?

2. What might be some negative consequences of the increased temperatures within an urban heat island?

 EVIDENCE NOTEBOOK As you explore the lesson, gather evidence to help explain the causes of urban heat islands.

Modeling the Flow of Thermal Energy through Systems

Energy Transfer

A radiometer, or light-mill, is a device that responds to light. When the radiometer is exposed to a bright light source, the vanes of the radiometer rotate.

The vanes of the radiometer are black on one side and silver on the other. The black surfaces absorb more energy from the light than the silver surfaces, so they become warmer. The gas particles near the black sides of the vanes warm up more than the gas particles near the silver sides. This increase in temperature indicates an increase in kinetic energy. This means the gas particles near the black sides of the vanes collide with the vanes more frequently and with more energy than the cooler gas particles on the silver sides do. The transfer of energy from the collisions causes the vanes of the radiometer to spin.

3. What is the energy input to the radiometer system? What form(s) of energy are present in the system as a result?

The vanes of a radiometer spin when they are exposed to bright light.

A transfer of energy happens when the energy in an object is added to or removed from that object. You can think of the entire radiometer as a **system**, or a set of interacting parts that work together. The vanes of the radiometer move because of a transfer of electromagnetic energy from a light source into the radiometer system.

The *law of conservation of energy* states that energy cannot be created or destroyed. The total energy of a system will increase if the input of energy from outside the system is greater than its output. Once a system's boundaries are defined, the inputs and outputs of energy can be modeled. The bulb is the boundary of the radiometer system. When the radiometer is exposed to a bright light source, the input of electromagnetic energy will be greater than the loss of thermal energy from the system.

EVIDENCE NOTEBOOK

4. Think about the energy inputs and outputs in an urban area. How do urban heat islands demonstrate the law of conservation of energy? Record your evidence.

The Flow of Thermal Energy

Thermal energy is a measure of the total kinetic energy of the particles in an object. This energy can flow as heat between parts of a system. Thermal energy is transferred three ways: conduction, convection, and radiation. Thermal energy is transferred by *conduction* when particles collide. *Convection* describes the transfer of thermal energy through the motion of particles of a fluid. In *radiation*, energy is transferred when electromagnetic waves are emitted by a warmer object and absorbed by a cooler object. Thermal energy always spontaneously flows from objects at higher temperatures to objects at lower temperatures.

Models of Thermal Energy Transfer in Systems

During the operation of a nuclear reactor, fuel rods in the reactor core produce a large amount of thermal energy. This energy is used to generate electrical energy. This energy is transferred to homes, schools, and businesses. After the used fuel rods are removed from a nuclear reactor, they are still very hot. These hot fuel rods are stored in cooling pools filled with water. Thermal energy from the hot fuel rods is transferred to the cooler water. As the fuel rods cool down, the temperature of the water in the pool increases. The rods eventually cool to just above the temperature of the warming water in the pool. Because the rods continue to produce thermal energy, they will always be a little warmer than the water.

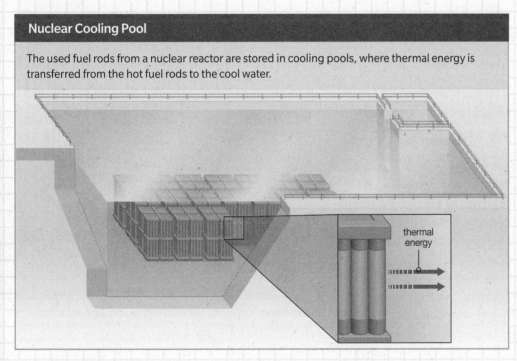

Nuclear Cooling Pool

The used fuel rods from a nuclear reactor are stored in cooling pools, where thermal energy is transferred from the hot fuel rods to the cool water.

thermal energy

5. How would the temperatures of the components of this system change if additional hot fuel rods were placed in the pool after a steady temperature was reached?

A. The temperature of the water and the original fuel rods would decrease.

B. The temperature of the water and the original fuel rods would increase.

C. The temperature of the water would decrease but the temperature of the original fuel rods would not change.

D. The temperature of the water would increase but the temperature of the original fuel rods would not change.

Thermal Energy Transfer and Ambient Temperature

All parts of a system will eventually reach the same temperature if there are no inputs or outputs of energy. The temperature of an object's surroundings is called the *ambient temperature*. For example, a building is a system surrounded by the ambient outdoor environment. If thermal energy is not added to the building, the indoor temperature will eventually become the same as the ambient outdoor temperature. If you light a fire in a fireplace, the building will become warmer than the ambient outdoor temperature.

Without energy inputs, the buildings will cool down to the ambient temperature.

6. Think of a window in a house as a system boundary separating the air on opposite sides of the glass pane. Draw the flow of thermal energy through the window when the indoor temperature is 23 °C and the outdoor temperature is 15 °C. Then show how the system model would change if the temperature outside were warmer than inside. How would bright sunshine affect the system?

Analyze Solar Heaters

Hot water from the faucets in your school is warmer than water that comes into the building from the water supply. Most water heaters use a combustible fuel, such as natural gas, or electrical energy to raise the water temperature. Solar water heaters raise the temperature of water by converting electromagnetic energy from the sun into thermal energy. These water heaters are generally placed on the roof of the building. After it is warmed, water flows to a hot water tank inside the building.

These solar water heaters convert electromagnetic energy into thermal energy.

7. Sometimes, the hot water produced by a solar water heater is not warm enough to meet the needs of the occupants of a building. A traditional water heater inside the building supplies additional thermal energy to the solar-warmed water. How can this method still reduce the overall amount of natural gas or electrical energy a building uses?

_____

_____

_____

_____

Describing the Thermal Properties of Materials

Pastry chefs around the world bake pies in plates with a similar shape, but they disagree on the best material for the plates. Some bakers claim they get the best results from shiny aluminum plates. Some chefs never use any material other than glass. A third group argues that ceramic is definitely the way to go.

8. Why might the material of a pie plate have an effect on the quality of the pie's crust?

A common problem when baking pies is burnt crust.

The Thermal Energy of an Object

The thermal energy of an object is the total kinetic energy of its particles. An object's thermal energy depends on the mass of the object, its temperature, its state of matter, and its chemical composition. Larger objects have more thermal energy than smaller objects of the same material and density at the same temperature. A liquid substance has more thermal energy than the same mass of the substance in its solid form.

9. Suppose you have two identical objects made of the same mass of the same material. If one object is 20 °C warmer than the other, which object has more thermal energy?

10. Suppose you have two objects made of the same material but with different masses. If both objects are the same temperature, which object has more thermal energy?

The amount of thermal energy an object has increases as its temperature increases because its particles are moving faster. A greater mass of the same substance at the same temperature will also contain more thermal energy. This is because it contains more moving particles. The composition of the object also affects the thermal energy because some materials are more likely to absorb thermal energy than others. Thermal energy is also related to a material's physical state, or phase. When a solid reaches its melting point or a liquid reaches its boiling point, its physical state changes.

Hands-On Lab

Examine the Transfer of Thermal Energy through Radiation

In this activity, you will investigate how the composition of an object affects its absorption of thermal energy through radiation.

Procedure and Analysis

STEP 1 Use a graduated cylinder to measure and pour the same amount of water into each of the two cans. The cans should be almost full.

STEP 2 Place a plastic foam cover on each can and insert a thermometer through the hole in the cover. Measure the temperature of the water in each can and record the value at time zero in the data table. The water in both cans should be approximately the same temperature.

STEP 3 Use the ruler to place each lamp the same distance from both cans. Turn on both lamps at the same time and begin timing the experiment.

STEP 4 Record the temperature of the water in both cans every 5 minutes for 30 minutes. On a separate piece of paper, graph your data showing the temperature of the water in each can over time.

STEP 5 Describe your observations about each can's absorption of radiation. Why does the water in the two cans have different temperatures at the end of the experiment?

MATERIALS
• adjustable desk lamps, each with at least 60-watt incandescent light bulbs (2)
• graduated cylinder, 100 mL
• plastic foam disks that can fit onto the tops of cans, each with a hole in the middle for a thermometer (2)
• ruler
• stopwatch or timer
• thermometers (2)
• tin cans of the same size (2), one painted matte black and the other painted matte white
• water

	Temperature (°C)	
Time (min)	White can	Black can
0		
5		
10		
15		
20		
25		
30		

EVIDENCE NOTEBOOK

11. How could the surfaces and structures in an urban area be related to the urban heat island effect? Record your evidence.

Changes in Thermal Energy

The total thermal energy of a particular component of a system depends on its temperature, mass, composition, and physical state. Different parts of a system can have different temperatures. Differences in thermal energy and temperature affect the transfer of energy to and from the system, as well as within the system. For example, water is able to absorb more thermal energy than the same amount of soil or rock. So, the temperature of land near large bodies of water is influenced by the temperature of the water.

The California current is a cold ocean current that runs south along the coast of California. During the summer this current becomes colder due to stronger global winds from the northwest. At the same time, air above the Central Valley is being heated by energy from the sun. Lower pressure over land leads to the wind blowing from west to east. This brings the moist air from over the Pacific Ocean toward California. The moist air is cooled by the California current. As the water vapor cools it condenses onto particles of salt in the air to form a thick layer of fog. The winds from the west often push this fog bank through the Golden Gate Bridge and into San Francisco Bay.

Fog forms in the San Francisco Bay area when moist air is cooled by a cold ocean current.

12. Different materials absorb and release thermal energy at different rates. How might you use this property to control the temperatures of components within a system?

The Thermal Properties of Substances

Think about baking something in a hot oven. When you take the pan out of the oven, you use a padded cloth potholder to hold the hot dish. Could you use a sheet of aluminum foil as a potholder? That would not be a good idea. It is likely that you would burn your hands. How an object absorbs and transfers thermal energy depends on the materials from which it is made. Some substances transfer thermal energy better than others. Aluminum foil rapidly transfers thermal energy from the pan to your hand. The cloth potholder does not.

You can also observe how different materials absorb and transfer thermal energy by touching a bicycle sitting in the sun on a hot summer day. The metal frame of the bike feels much hotter than the plastic handlebar grips. Metals, such as aluminum or steel, transfer thermal energy to your hand much faster than plastic.

Engineers consider differences in properties of materials during the design process. Because some materials conduct heat better than others, heat will flow differently depending on the materials used. The transfer of thermal energy to and from an object does not just depend on the difference between the temperatures of the object and its surroundings. It also depends on the material from which the object is made.

Differences in Thermal Energy Transfer

Aluminum, glass, and ceramic each transfer thermal energy differently. The table shows the thermal conductivity values for these materials. Thermal conductivity is a measure of how quickly a material transfers thermal energy, measured in watts per meter-Kelvin (W/m•K). The higher the value, the faster the material transfers energy.

The values in the table indicate that an aluminum pie plate will conduct heat much more quickly than a glass or ceramic plate. This means that thermal energy will transfer to the pie crust through conduction faster in an aluminum plate. A glass pie plate will conduct heat much more slowly. Because glass is clear, the transfer of radiant thermal energy will be greater in the glass plate than in the ceramic plate. Even though ceramic has a higher thermal conductivity value, a ceramic plate is likely to cook the crust more slowly than a glass plate. It does not transfer thermal energy by radiation.

13. **Discuss** Based on the thermal properties of aluminum, glass, and ceramic, how would you revise your recommendation for a pie-plate material? Would one material be preferable to the others based on the pie you are baking?

Thermal Conductivities	
Substance	**Thermal conductivity (W/m•K)**
Aluminum	205
Ceramic	1.5
Glass	1.1
Stainless steel	16

Engineer It
Analyze Evaporative Cooling

The thermal energy of a substance is related to its physical state. The particles of a gas move faster than those of a liquid. So, the gas carries more thermal energy compared to the same amount of liquid.

In dry climates, people often use evaporative coolers instead of air conditioners. In an evaporative cooling system, water is added to an evaporative pad. A fan pulls hot, dry air from the outside through the damp pad and into the building. The water in the damp pad changes from liquid to gas by absorbing some thermal energy from the hot, dry air. As the air loses thermal energy to the water, it becomes cooler.

Evaporative Cooler

14. Add the following labels in the correct spaces below to complete this general model of an evaporative cooling system. HD for hot, dry air and CM for cool, dry air.

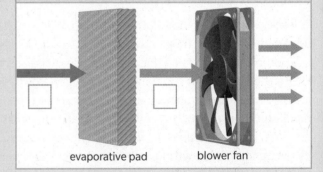

evaporative pad   blower fan

EVIDENCE NOTEBOOK

15. As plants grow, they release water vapor into the atmosphere around them. How might this be related to urban landscapes and surrounding areas? Record your evidence.

Applying the Concepts of Heat Transfer

The application of the transfer of thermal energy in real-world situations is often referred to as *heat transfer*. Engineers are often required to develop solutions to control heat transfer. For example, greenhouses are designed to maximize the amount of *radiant* thermal energy taken in during sunny hours. They also minimize the amount of *convective* thermal energy lost to the atmosphere at night. One way to store thermal energy is to use a thermal mass.

A *thermal mass* is a material that absorbs thermal energy when the air around it is warmer, and then slowly releases it when the air is cooler. Many greenhouses use big black barrels filled with water for this purpose. The barrels absorb thermal energy during the day and release thermal energy during the night.

In this greenhouse, the concrete floor acts as a thermal mass by absorbing radiant energy during the day and slowly releasing it after sundown.

Identify a Heat Transfer Problem: Design a Safe Lunch Carrier

People sometimes call a lunch that someone carries to work or school a "brown bag" lunch, but a paper bag is not always a safe way to carry food. Some foods must be kept cold to be safe, such as meats, cheeses, milk, sliced fruits, or salads. Bacteria that can make you sick grow quickly when the temperature of the food is between 4 °C and 60 °C. That means that the food carrier must keep chilled food almost as cold as a refrigerator at home. Hot food must stay above 60 °C to be safe.

The engineering process begins with defining the engineering problem. In this case, the problem is to design a container that keeps chilled food at a safe temperature long enough to last until lunch.

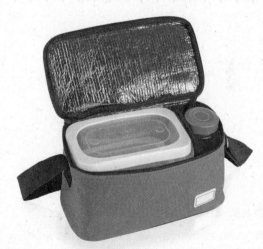

Insulated containers for hot and cold foods can help to keep packed lunches safe.

The next step in the engineering design process is to precisely define the criteria and constraints of an acceptable solution. The *criteria* for the problem are the properties that the product should have in order to successfully solve the problem. Think about what the container should do in order to solve the problem in this situation. *Constraints* are limitations on the solution. For example, a small refrigerator might meet the criterion of keeping food cold. It would not be a successful solution if there is a constraint that the container must be portable.

Define the Criteria

Because this engineering problem involves heat transfer, an important criterion is whether the heat transfer should be maximized or minimized. In this case, the goal is to minimize heat transfer. You can begin defining the criteria for this engineering problem by stating that the solution should reduce heat transfer as much as possible. Another criterion might be to make sure that any heat transfer that does happen will occur slowly. A specific statement could be that the solution will hold a chilled lunch that starts at 2 °C for five hours at a temperature of 7 °C or below.

16. The goals of the design are not only to minimize heat transfer. Because this is a design for a carrier for taking lunch to school, you might want to consider other criteria, such as appearance and size. What are some criteria that you would include to define the problem more precisely?

17. Consider your list of criteria for a lunch carrier design. Think about the purpose of the designed product. Which criterion is the most important one you should consider for possible solutions?

Define the Constraints

Along with its criteria, every engineering problem has constraints. Identifying the constraints helps you think about possible solutions more realistically. What kind of constraints might apply to a lunch carrier engineering problem? They might include the availability of materials, the amount of money that you have to spend, safety considerations, and environmental or societal impacts.

18. Discuss What are some of the constraints of the lunch container problem?

Design Heat Transfer Solutions

After you have clearly defined the problem and determined its criteria and constraints, you can begin to work on a solution. It is often helpful to brainstorm possible solutions based on background research. Before designing a safe lunch container, think about the thermal properties of different common materials you could use to construct a container. You have already identified minimizing heat transfer as an important criterion of the problem.

Do the Math
Compare Thermal Properties of Different Materials

Some materials transfer thermal energy very quickly. These materials are called *thermal conductors*. Other materials, known as *thermal insulators*, transfer energy slowly. The thermal conductivity values shown in this table compare how quickly the materials transfer heat. Recall that materials with higher thermal conductivity values transfer thermal energy more quickly than materials with lower thermal conductivity values.

Thermal Conductivities of Substances	
Substance	Thermal conductivity (W/m•K)
Aluminum	205
Cloth (wool)	0.07
Copper	401
Polyethylene plastic	0.42
Polystyrene foam	0.03
Tin	67
Wood (pine)	0.12

19. Based on the data in the table above, which materials might work the best in designing a safe lunch container? Use evidence to explain your answer.

20. **Collaborate** With a group, use information from the text and your own experiences to brainstorm design solutions. Besides the thermal properties of the materials you use to build your lunch container, consider other design features that might be important for your solution. Record every suggestion made by your group members.

Choose the Best Solutions

After brainstorming, your group will have a number of ideas that can be used for solutions. Some of them will be more likely to solve the problem than others. Now evaluate and critique each possible solution. First, eliminate any solutions that violate the constraints of the problem. Next, compare how successfully the remaining solutions meet the criteria.

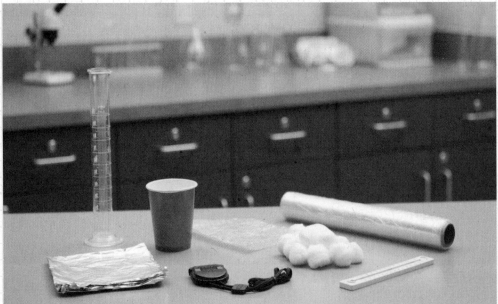

Some materials will perform better as thermal insulators than others. Testing a model will help to develop a solution.

Develop and Test a Model

Once you have determined that one or more of the solutions best meets the criteria and constraints, you need to test those solutions. In order to test solutions, you need to develop a model for each proposed solution. This model can be an actual device, a scale model, or a computer model. You also need to develop a method for testing how well the solution meets the design requirements. The test method should ensure that you obtain accurate data for comparing results.

Hands-On Lab
Design and Test an Insulated Container

You will design a device to insulate a paper cup containing ice-cold water. After you design the device, you will build a model and test it by measuring the change in water temperature over a period of 30 minutes.

The engineering problem is to design a system that minimizes the transfer of thermal energy to the water from its surroundings. In this case, the criteria and constraints include the use of available materials and completion of the design and construction of the model in the time designated by your teacher.

Procedure and Analysis

STEP 1 With your group, brainstorm ideas for building an insulation system to minimize change in temperature of the water in the cup.

STEP 2 Evaluate the solutions that were suggested during the brainstorming session. During evaluation, you may want to eliminate some ideas. You may also want to combine parts of two or more ideas. Then build a model of the selected solution for testing.

STEP 3 Test your model by measuring 150 mL of ice-cold water into the cup and placing the cup in the model. Be careful not to include any ice in the water. Measure the temperature of the water, and record it as time zero on the data table.

STEP 4 After 5 minutes, measure and record the temperature of the water. Repeat every 5 minutes for 30 minutes.

STEP 5 What did you observe during your investigation? How do your data show that a transfer of thermal energy did or did not occur?

MATERIALS
- aluminum foil
- bubble packing
- cardboard
- cotton balls
- cotton fabric
- drinking straws
- graduated cylinder, 100 mL or larger
- ice
- paper cup
- plastic film
- rubber bands
- sheets of paper
- stopwatch or timer
- string
- thermometer
- water
- wire
- other materials provided by your teacher

Thermal Energy Transfer Data

Time (min)	Temperature (°C)
0	
5	
10	
15	
20	
25	
30	

Analyze and Revise the Design

After completing the test, you need to analyze the data resulting from the test of the design solution. Compare your results with others in the class. Evaluate how different design solutions performed. With your group, discuss how each aspect of the design may have contributed to its success or failure.

 21. Language SmArts Based on your analysis, suggest some modifications to improve your container. Support your argument using evidence from your experiment and the text.

Analyze Geothermal Heat Pumps

Geothermal technology uses the transfer of thermal energy to or from the ground beneath a structure. Just a few feet below the ground's surface, the temperature is almost constant all year long. Geothermal heat pumps take advantage of the difference between the above-ground air temperature and the soil temperature below the surface to warm and cool buildings. A liquid is pumped through underground pipes. To warm a room, the pump transfers thermal energy from the liquid to the building's heating system. Then the cooled liquid flows through the pipes underground where thermal energy flows into it again before returning to the indoor heating system. For cooling, the heat pump adds thermal energy to the liquid, which is cooled underground.

22. Geothermal heat pumps require a lot less energy than traditional heating and air conditioning systems. How do the energy inputs and outputs differ between a house with a heat pump and a house with a furnace that burns fuel? Explain why using this technology could lead to a reduction of the issues associated with urban heat islands and other problems.

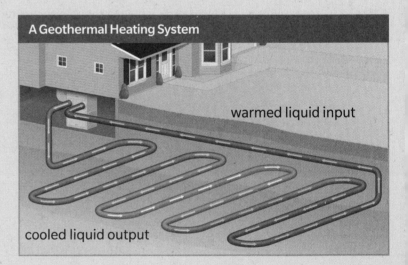

A Geothermal Heating System

warmed liquid input

cooled liquid output

_____

_____

_____

_____

_____

Continue Your Exploration

Name: _____   Date: _____

Check out the path below or go online to choose one of the other paths shown.

> **Careers in Engineering**
>
> • **Maximizing Heat Transfer**
> • **Hands-On Labs** ✋
> • **Propose Your Own Path**
>
> *Go online to choose one of these other paths.*

Energy Conservationist

Many modern systems such as buildings, transportation networks, and lighting systems consume a lot of energy. This energy usage is expensive, consumes a large amount of natural resources, and causes pollution that contributes to global climate change. Energy conservationists work to develop solutions to reduce energy consumption.

An energy conservationist may also be an engineer, an environmental scientist, or a building designer. The main goal of the job is to increase the efficiency of systems so they use less energy but still function well. To do this, the energy conservationist has to understand how energy is generated and transmitted and how it is used in the system. The best solution to the problem of energy conservation often saves money, even if it requires new equipment. Energy conservationists have to find ways to save energy in industries such as hotels, commercial properties, municipalities, and even in private homes. Then they make recommendations to solve the engineering design problem of reducing energy consumption.

An energy conservationist measures energy usage and designs ways to reduce it.

1. An energy conservationist often works as a consultant who makes recommendations that other people use to make decisions. What type of information would the energy conservationist have to consider in order to convince people that changes are a good idea?

Continue Your Exploration

An Energy-Efficient Home

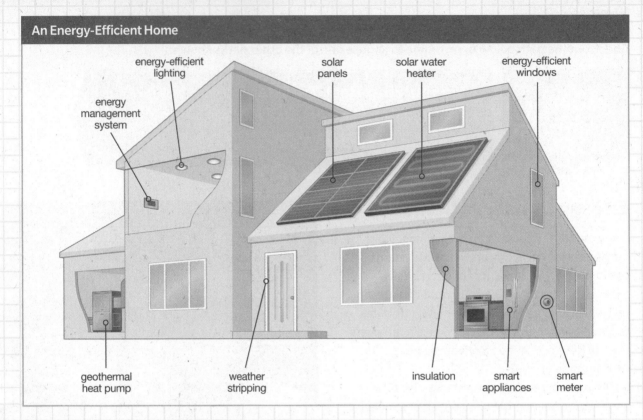

One way to improve home energy usage is to use renewable resources such as solar energy or geothermal energy and to reduce fuel usage. Another approach is to reduce energy use. Efficient appliances, insulation, and well-designed windows and doors reduce impacts on the environment and the costs of providing energy.

2. Which of these changes might be suggested by an energy conservationist to reduce the transfer of thermal energy to a home's surroundings? Select all that apply.

A. Add more insulation to the attic of the home.

B. Use renewable energy sources instead of fossil fuels to heat the home.

C. Install the most energy-efficient appliances available.

3. An energy conservationist studies a home and makes a suggestion that each room should have a separate thermostat instead of having one temperature control device in a central room. How could this suggestion help reduce energy usage in the home?

4. Collaborate Discuss with a group how you and your families can be "energy conservationists" in your own everyday lives. What steps do you take to make sure your use of energy is most efficient? As a group, make a poster showing things that you can do to minimize your energy use and share your ideas with the class.

Can You Explain It?

Name: _____   **Date:** _____

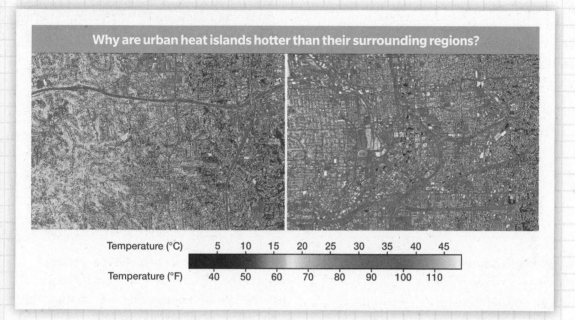

Why are urban heat islands hotter than their surrounding regions?

Temperature (°C)   5   10   15   20   25   30   35   40   45

Temperature (°F)   40   50   60   70   80   90   100   110

 EVIDENCE NOTEBOOK

Refer to the notes in your Evidence Notebook to help you construct an explanation for the causes of urban heat islands.

1. State your claim. Make sure your claim fully explains why urban heat islands are hotter than their surrounding regions.

2. Summarize the evidence you have gathered to support your claim and explain your reasoning.

Checkpoints

Answer the following questions to check your understanding of the lesson.

Use the table to answer Question 3.

3. When you cook food by stir-frying, it is important to transfer thermal energy to the food as quickly as possible. Which of these metals would be the best choice for a pan intended for stir-frying vegetables?

   A. aluminum

   B. copper

   C. stainless steel

   D. tin

Thermal Conductivities of Substances	
Substance	Thermal conductivity (W/m•K)
Aluminum	205
Cloth (wool)	0.07
Copper	401
Polyethylene	0.42
Polystyrene foam	0.03
Stainless steel	16
Tin	67
Wood (pine)	0.12

4. Why would a light-colored roof be preferable to a dark roof in a warm, sunny area?

   A. The dark-colored roof will not cool the house as quickly at nighttime.

   B. The dark-colored roof absorbs more energy during the day and becomes hotter.

   C. The light-colored roof absorbs more energy and keeps it from entering the house.

   D. The light-colored roof cools the house faster than the dark-colored roof.

5. If you place a hot piece of metal in a container of water, thermal energy flows from the metal to the water. What happens after the metal and the water reach the same temperature?

   A. The flow of thermal energy stops, and the temperature remains constant.

   B. The flow of thermal energy continues and causes both substances to become warmer.

   C. The flow of thermal energy reverses and causes both substances to become warmer.

   D. The flow of thermal energy reverses, and the water becomes colder.

Use the diagram to answer Question 6.

6. There are two streams of liquid flowing through the heat exchanger. As these streams pass opposite sides of the tubes, thermal energy transfers from Liquid A/ Liquid B to Liquid A/ Liquid B.

Liquid A output (60 °C)   Liquid B input (20 °C)

Liquid B output (35 °C)   Liquid A input (80 °C)

This diagram shows a heat exchanger used in a chemical processing plant. Thermal energy is transferred between the liquids flowing through the tubes in the exchanger.

Interactive Review

Complete this section to review the main concepts of the lesson.

Thermal energy flows from a warmer object or substance to a cooler object or substance. The total amount of thermal energy in a system does not change unless energy transfers into or out of the system.

A. How does the flow of thermal energy in a solid object change when it is taken from a warm building out into the cold?

The amount of thermal energy that a substance or object contains depends on its temperature, composition, physical state, and mass.

B. How does the thermal energy of a pie fresh out of the oven compare to the thermal energy of a pie fresh out of the refrigerator?

Thermal conductors transfer thermal energy faster than thermal insulators.

C. How is a thermal mass in a building similar to a large body of water, such as a lake?

Changes in Energy Drive the Water Cycle

A dark storm approaches a wooden structure built in the water in the Maldives.

Explore First

Collecting Water Remove a sealed container of water from a refrigerator where it had time to become cold to the touch. Place the container on a table and observe any changes. What is happening on the outside of the container? Where is the water coming from?

Go online to view the digital version of the Hands-On Lab for this lesson and to download additional lab resources.

CAN YOU EXPLAIN IT?

How could the water in a dinosaur's drink end up in a raindrop today?

Some of Earth's water makes up your body as well as the bodies of all living things. A tiny drop of water can contain more than a trillion water molecules. Every water molecule has its own story, and some water molecules at Earth's surface today may have been ingested by a dinosaur 200 million years ago.

1. Think about the last drink of water you took. How do you think that water may have moved or changed before you drank it?

2. How do you think the physical state of water affects its movement?

EVIDENCE NOTEBOOK As you explore the lesson, gather evidence to show how water in a dinosaur's drink could end up in a raindrop today.

Analyzing Water on Earth

Where Water Is Found on Earth

Water is found almost everywhere on Earth, and it exists in many forms. From space, it is easy to see Earth's oceans. They cover about 70% of Earth's surface. Salt water makes up about 97% of Earth's total volume of water. For humans and for many animals, the salt dissolved in seawater makes it too salty to drink. It is also too salty to use to water crops.

3. Together with a partner, look at the photo for evidence of water. Besides the oceans, where else is water present on Earth? Is it always in liquid form?

Earth is known as "the blue planet" because most of its surface is covered with water.

The Importance of Water on Earth

Water plays an important role in many processes in the Earth's system. It shapes Earth's surface and influences weather. Water is also essential for life. You depend on clean, fresh drinking water to survive. Only a limited amount of Earth's water—about 2.5%—is fresh water. The remaining water on Earth is salt water. Almost 70% of Earth's fresh water is frozen in ice and not readily available for us to use. Therefore, it is important to protect our water resources.

Water's Role on Earth

Water shapes Earth's surface through weathering and erosion, and it also influences Earth's weather.

Water is vital for sustaining all organisms on Earth.

4. **Discuss** Together with a partner or with your class, discuss at least four things you did or used today that would not be possible or would not exist without water.

States of Water on Earth

Earth is the only planet in our solar system with abundant liquid water. The Earth system also contains water in two other states: gas and solid. Water (liquid), water vapor (an invisible gas), and ice (solid) all have the same chemical formula of H_2O.

The States of Water

Liquid Most of Earth's water is liquid. Gravity causes liquid water to flow downhill and rest in low-lying areas. As a result, Earth has rivers, lakes, and oceans.

Gas Most water vapor is in Earth's atmosphere. We cannot see water vapor, but our bodies take it in every time we inhale.

Solid Solid water forms ice crystals, snowflakes, and hail in Earth's atmosphere and ice and snow on Earth's surface.

5. Look at the scene in the photo. Describe two ways that the liquid water you see here could have come to this location on Earth.

Water's Changing State

When the temperature of the environment that water is in rises, water can absorb thermal energy. As water absorbs energy, it can change from solid to liquid, from liquid to gas, or from solid to gas. The same amount of water that existed before the change of state exists after the change of state.

On the other hand, if the surrounding environment cools, water can lose energy to its surroundings and can change state in the opposite direction. As energy is released from water, the water may change from gas to liquid, from liquid to solid, or from gas to solid.

 EVIDENCE NOTEBOOK

6. Think back to the dinosaur's drinking water. Was this water always in the liquid state? Did it remain in a liquid state after the dinosaur drank it? Record your evidence.

7. In each image, fill in the blank to indicate whether water *gains* or *loses* kinetic energy.

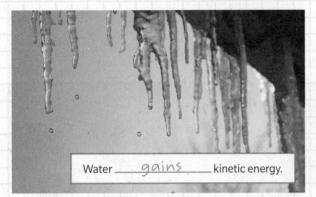

Water ___*gains*___ kinetic energy.

As air temperatures increase, the water molecules in this ice begin to vibrate just enough to break free and start to flow past one another to form a liquid.

Water _____ kinetic energy.

As air temperatures decrease, the molecules in liquid water begin to move more slowly until they only vibrate in place. The molecules form the rigid structure of solid water, or ice.

Water _____ kinetic energy.

As air temperatures increase, liquid water molecules begin to vibrate enough that some will escape the liquid's surface into the air above as water vapor.

Water _____ kinetic energy.

As water vapor molecules rise, they eventually enter colder air. This causes the molecules to vibrate at a slower rate and change to liquid water droplets.

Do the Math
Analyze Temperatures

When we find the temperature of something, we are really measuring the average kinetic energy of the particles in that object. The freezing point and the melting point of water are both 0 °C. When water cools to 0 °C or below, it is losing kinetic energy, and is likely to freeze. If ice warms to 0 °C or above, it is gaining kinetic energy and is likely to melt. And the boiling point of water is 100 °C.

8. In the United States and some other countries, temperature is generally measured in degrees Fahrenheit (°F). Scientists generally measure temperature in degrees Celsius (°C), so it is helpful to be familiar with both temperature scales. Use the equation to calculate the temperature in °F for each item below. The first one has been done for you.

$$F = \frac{9}{5}C + 32$$

a running stream	snow	boiling water
25 °C = 77 °F	0 °C =	100 °C =

Describing the Movement of Water in Earth's Atmosphere

A mixture of gases surrounds Earth and makes up its atmosphere. Earth's atmosphere contains nitrogen, carbon dioxide, oxygen, and water. At any given time there is about 12,900 km³ of water in the atmosphere. That's enough water to completely fill Lake Superior, the largest lake by volume in North America!

9. What evidence of water in the atmosphere can you see in the photo?

The atmosphere contains a lot of water vapor, which you cannot see.

How Water Reaches the Atmosphere

Water can exist in the atmosphere as a solid, a liquid, and a gas. In addition to evaporation, two other processes can move water into the atmosphere from Earth's surface. These processes are transpiration and sublimation.

10. Where can water in the atmosphere come from? Circle all possible answers.

   A. oceans

   B. plants

   C. ice

   D. puddles

When liquid water gains enough energy to escape the liquid's surface and form water vapor, the process is called **evaporation**. Some water evaporates from the water on land. However, most water evaporates from the surface of Earth's oceans. The amount of thermal energy needed to evaporate water from different parts of Earth's oceans depends on the kinetic energy of the ocean water. In some places, the ocean water is cold at the surface, and has less kinetic energy. Here, more thermal energy is needed for water to evaporate. In other places, the ocean water is warm at the surface and needs less thermal energy for evaporation to occur.

Ways Water Reaches the Atmosphere

sublimation

transpiration

evaporation

Liquid water is found in organisms' bodies. Water is ingested as an animal eats and drinks. Some water is stored in the animal's body and some is returned back into the environment by excretion or respiration. When an animal dies, its body decomposes and any water in the body is returned to the environment. Like many organisms, plants release water vapor into the environment. As water flows throughout a plant, some water changes to water vapor as it leaves the plant through small openings called stomata. This release of water vapor into the air by plants is called **transpiration**. This process requires the addition of kinetic energy to the water molecules, so they can break away from the liquid state.

When solid water changes directly to water vapor without first becoming a liquid, the process is called **sublimation**. Energy is required for this process to occur because the molecules of the solid water must gain enough kinetic energy to break free from the solid state.

How important are the contributions from each source of atmospheric water? About 90% of the water in the atmosphere comes from evaporation of Earth's liquid water, especially oceans. About 10% of the water in the atmosphere comes from transpiration. Less than 1% of the water in the atmosphere comes from sublimation.

Water in the Atmosphere

Water molecules in the atmosphere are in constant motion, bouncing against each other and against other gas molecules in the air. During these collisions, the water molecules spontaneously gain or lose kinetic energy. If a water molecule collides with a molecule that is warmer, and so has more kinetic energy, the water molecule will gain kinetic energy. If a water molecule collides with a molecule that is cooler, and so has less kinetic energy, the water molecule will lose kinetic energy.

EVIDENCE NOTEBOOK

11. Through what processes might the water have changed and moved before and after the dinosaur drank it? Record your evidence.

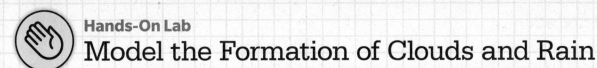

Hands-On Lab
Model the Formation of Clouds and Rain

You will model Earth's atmosphere inside a jar.

Procedure and Analysis

STEP 1 Carefully fill a jar about half full by pouring 250 mL of hot water into it.

STEP 2 Place a dented lid on top of the jar so that it covers the entire opening and the raised bumps are facing down into the jar.

STEP 3 Place ice cubes, a little cold water, and a teaspoon of salt into the can and stir. Put the cold can on top of the lid of the jar.

STEP 4 Shine a flashlight through the jar. Record your observations. Repeat this step every few minutes for 10 minutes.

STEP 5 Use what you observed in this activity to explain some of the things that can happen to water in Earth's atmosphere. What might cause these changes?

MATERIALS
- can, empty
- flashlight
- ice cubes
- glass jar, medium size with a dented lid
- salt (1 tsp)
- water, very hot (250 mL)
- water, cold

Condensation and Clouds

As air cools, water vapor in the air may change to liquid water. The process of a gas becoming a liquid is called **condensation**. As water molecules bump into each other, they can stick together and form small water droplets or ice crystals, depending on the air temperature. At first, these droplets form around tiny particles in the air, such as sea salt, dust, and pollen. As more and more water molecules collect in the water droplets, the droplets become larger. Eventually, there may be enough water droplets to form visible clouds, fog, or mist.

High clouds that form at temperatures colder than those close to Earth's surface are made up of solid ice crystals and liquid droplets. At the ground level, water vapor may condense as dew or frost on cool surfaces, such as blades of grass and windows.

12. Microscopic droplets of water in the air grow larger as water vapor continues to condense. What might happen next?

Precipitation

As the water droplets in clouds become larger and larger, the pull of gravity on them increases. Eventually, the force of gravity can cause the water in clouds to fall to Earth's surface. **Precipitation** is any form of water that falls to Earth from clouds. Three common kinds of precipitation are rain, snow, and hail. Snow and hail form when the water in clouds freezes.

Hailstones are frozen balls of precipitation that form in some thunderstorms.

You can see the beautiful six-part crystals of snowflakes when they are viewed under magnification.

Rain falls when water droplets that form in clouds are pulled to Earth's surface by gravity.

Deposition

Deposition occurs when water vapor changes state directly from a gas to a solid. Deposition is the reverse of sublimation. One example of deposition occurs high in the atmosphere or on the top of high mountains where the temperature is very low. In these conditions, water vapor forms snow without becoming a liquid first.

13. Circle the best answer to complete each statement.

   A. When water vapor in the atmosphere condenses and forms water droplets, the water molecules *absorb / release* energy.

   B. When liquid water in the atmosphere form ice crystals, the water molecules *absorb / release* energy.

Describe the Formation of Hail

Sometimes, when ice crystals form in clouds and begin to fall, strong winds carry the ice crystals high into the clouds. When the crystals begin falling again, they grow larger as more water droplets freeze onto them. Clumps of ice, called hailstones, start to form. Eventually, the hailstones grow too heavy for the wind to carry and they fall to Earth.

14. Describe a time during the formation of hailstones when water releases energy.

_____

_____

_____

_____

_____

_____

_____

Describing the Movement of Water on Earth's Surface

Much of Earth's surface is covered with water. Most of this water is salt water, which makes up Earth's oceans, salt marshes, and salty lakes. Only a small amount of Earth's water is fresh water, and most of that is frozen as sea ice at the poles or as ice and snow on land.

15. From photos of Earth's surface can you see all the locations where water might be? Explain.

The Dungeness River in Washington State forks before entering the bay and the Strait of Juan de Fuca.

Ocean Circulation

While it is easy to observe water flowing on land after a rainstorm, remember that most of Earth's precipitation falls into the ocean. Just as water moves through Earth's rivers, water in the ocean also moves in patterns. The movement of ocean water in a particular direction and pattern is called a *current*. This diagram shows the main pattern of ocean circulation, but does not show all ocean currents. The light green paths show currents on the ocean surface. The dark green paths show currents below the surface.

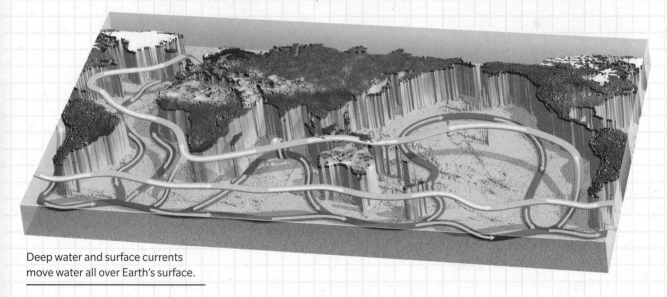

Deep water and surface currents move water all over Earth's surface.

16. In which ways might ocean currents be like streams and rivers on land?

Surface Currents and Deep Ocean Currents

Currents at or near the ocean surface are called *surface currents*. Surface currents are powered by wind. The wind is powered by thermal energy from the sun. The Gulf Stream, which moves warm ocean water from the Gulf of Mexico northeast toward Europe, is one example of a surface current. As this current moves toward Europe, it also moves the thermal energy found in the water.

Currents that flow below the ocean surface are called deep currents. These currents are driven by differences in water densities. Gravity causes denser water to sink below surrounding water in some parts of the ocean.

Deep currents flow at all levels of the ocean below the surface. Ocean currents transport large amounts of water as well as dissolved solids, dissolved gases, organisms, and energy around the Earth system.

Water Movement on Land

Water from the atmosphere falls to Earth's surface in the form of precipitation. Some precipitation forms coverings of snow and ice on mountains and other cold places. When this ice and snow melts, and when rain falls, the liquid water flows downhill. Some of the water may seep into the ground.

In the Highlands of Scotland, mountain streams flow down to lower elevations. As the water flows downhill it loses potential energy and gains kinetic energy.

17. What drives the movement of water in Earth's systems?

Runoff and Infiltration

Just as gravity pulls you and all other objects toward Earth's center, it also pulls on water. So, when precipitation lands on Earth's surface, some of the water will flow downhill across Earth's surface into wetlands, rivers, or lakes. Water that flows across Earth's surface this way is called **runoff**.

Some of the water on land may also seep below Earth's surface into spaces in soil and rock. This process is called *infiltration*. Water under Earth's surface is called *groundwater*. Groundwater can flow downhill through soil and some types of rock. Some drinking water in the United States comes from groundwater supplies. To use these supplies, people drill down into the ground to reach the groundwater. More than 75% of Earth's fresh water exists as ice and about 20% exists as groundwater.

Water Movement on and below Earth's Surface

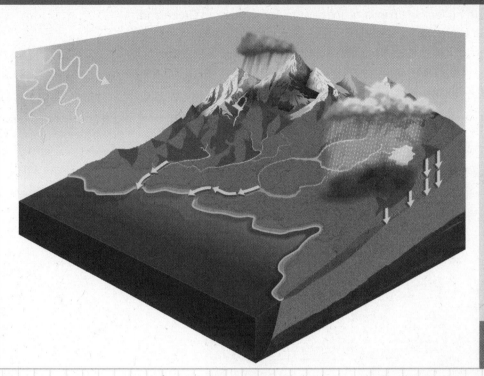

Water flows over Earth's surface as runoff from precipitation, melting snow, and ice. Some of this water flows through streams and rivers. Because of gravity, some of this water seeps downward to form groundwater.

Explore Online

18. Which statement correctly describes the movement of water represented by arrows in the picture? Choose all that apply.

A. Water from melting snow runs down the mountainside.

B. Rainwater seeps into the ground.

C. Streams carry water to the mountain peaks.

D. Gravity prevents groundwater from reaching Earth's surface.

19. Engineer It In some rivers and lakes, dams are constructed to harvest energy by converting the mechanical energy of moving water into electrical energy. Dams also form reservoirs that can be used to supply fresh water, which is a valuable resource in California.

    These reservoirs also disrupt natural systems and cycles. Ecosystems upstream are flooded and destroyed. Downstream, ecosystems that depend on seasonal flooding can suffer from a lack of water. What kinds of trade-offs need to be considered before construction of a freshwater reservoir can begin? Explain your reasoning.

Dams, such as the Glen Canyon Dam, can help control water movement on Earth's surface.

Ice on Earth's Surface

Most of Earth's fresh water is locked up in large ice caps in Antarctica and Greenland, or in ice floating in polar ocean water. Some ice is also found in glaciers. Glaciers are sometimes called "rivers of ice" because gravity causes them to move slowly downhill. Many glaciers never leave land. However, some glaciers reach the ocean, where pieces may break off and form icebergs.

Glacier Bay National Park, Alaska, is home to large glaciers that have carried ice over the land for thousands of years. This glacier flows to the ocean.

20. How might an iceberg move once it breaks off from a glacier?

Analyze Processes

21. Which of the following processes could have caused this cave to fill with water?

  A. evaporation

  B. sublimation

  C. infiltration

  D. transpiration

22. Together with a partner, think of a way water might exit this cave. Explain your reasoning.

A limestone cave beneath Earth's surface can fill with water over time.

_____

_____

_____

_____

_____

_____

_____

Modeling the Water Cycle

You can use everyday experiences to observe and model the movement of water in Earth's systems. You can observe some changes in water after any hot shower you take. While much of the shower water goes down the drain, some evaporates into the bathroom air. You know this because the mirror fogs up as that water vapor condenses back into liquid. When returning to the bathroom after a day at school, you notice that the mirror and your wet towel are now dry. Think about what happened to the water.

Time

23. **Discuss** Together with a partner, examine the photos. The material inside the glass changes over time. What do you think happened? Did the ice and water just disappear?

The Water Cycle

On a global scale, water constantly moves through Earth's system. The movement of water among the atmosphere, land, oceans, and living things is called the **water cycle**. This cycling of water involves changes of state, the movement of water in different forms, and the transfer of matter and energy in Earth's system.

A Water Cycle Model

24. Complete the water cycle model by writing the correct process in the spaces provided. Write *condensation, runoff, infiltration,* or *evaporation.*

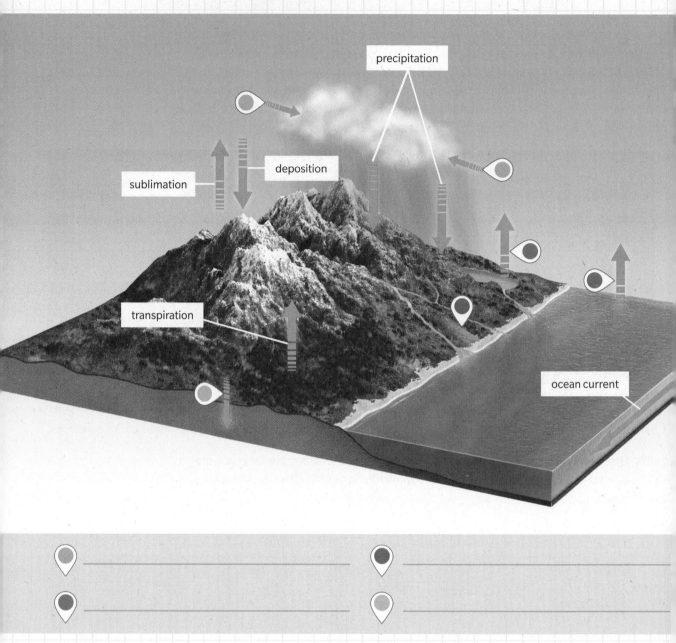

25. What other processes that involve energy in Earth's system are not shown in this model of the water cycle?

Sunlight and Gravity Drive the Water Cycle

Surface water, groundwater, and ice flow downhill because of gravity. Precipitation falls to Earth's surface because of gravity. Energy from the sun is the source of changes of state in which water absorbs energy, such as melting and evaporation. Solar energy also powers Earth's winds, which move air and water in the atmosphere.

26. Describe what might happen in the water cycle if the amount of solar energy entering the Earth system decreased.

The Flow of Energy in the Water Cycle

Energy flows through the Earth's system in the water cycle in two ways—when water changes state and when water moves from place to place. When water changes state, water molecules absorb energy from or release energy to their surroundings. For example, water can evaporate when it absorbs energy from sunlight or from surrounding air, water, or land. When water condenses to form clouds, the water molecules release energy to the surrounding atmosphere.

As water moves, it transfers energy from one location to another. For example, as a warm surface current in the ocean flows to a colder polar region, thermal energy from the equator is transported toward Earth's poles. When the warm water reaches areas where the air is colder, some energy in the warmer water is released into the cooler air. These energy transfers between the ocean and the atmosphere greatly influence Earth's weather and climate.

27. Imagine snow on top of a mountain. What are some ways energy could be transferred as the seasons change? Choose all answers that apply.

A. Energy flows into the snow from sunlight.

B. Cold snow melt flows into the warmer lake.

C. Warmer air absorbs energy from snow.

D. Energy flows into the snow from warmer air.

The Cycling of Matter in the Water Cycle

As water moves above, on top of, and below Earth's surface, it carries other matter with it. For example, streams and rivers carry sand, mud, and living things, which are deposited in a new place. As water moves over land, some substances will dissolve in the water and be carried along with it. When the water evaporates, the dissolved substances will be deposited. Precipitation can carry substances from the air to the ground, including gases, dust, ash, pollen, and pollutants.

28. What are some other examples of the cycling of matter that happen as a result of the water cycle?

29. How could a water molecule move through the water cycle over millions of years? Record your evidence.

Model the Water Cycle

The movement of water throughout Earth's systems is called the water cycle. However, this cycle is not a "circle" of events. A water molecule can take different paths as it moves through the cycle. The term *cycle* refers to the fact that water continuously moves from Earth's surface to the atmosphere and back.

30. Language SmArts Remember the water on the bathroom mirror that appears after you take a shower? Tell a story about how those droplets appear on the mirror and what could happen to a water molecule from one of the droplets as it moves through the water cycle. Describe at least four changes in the state of water, the processes that move the water, and how energy flows to and from the water. Be sure to include at least one living organism in the water cycle.

_____

_____

_____

_____

_____

_____

_____

31. Draw In the space below, draw a model to go with your story. Use arrows and labels to show processes in the water cycle. Present your story and model to the class.

Continue Your Exploration

Name: Date:

Check out the path below or go online to choose one of the other paths shown.

Careers in Science

- **People in Science**
- **Investigating Water Sources**
- **Hands-On Labs**
- **Propose Your Own Path**

Go online to choose one of these other paths.

Hydrologist

Hydrologists are scientists who study water. They study a wide variety of topics, including water quality and availability. Some hydrologists also study water's movement at different scales, from global ocean currents to local replenishment of reservoirs by spring snowmelt. Hydrologists use many instruments in their work, including depth gauges and flow meters.

Hydrologists take water samples along irrigation channels near the Rio Grande. They are looking for pharmaceuticals, nutrients, metals, and other characteristics to determine water quality.

Continue Your Exploration

The Rio Grande runs along the border between Texas and Mexico. The river is an important resource. It is a vital stop along birds' migration routes. It is central to many important desert ecosystems, and houses several dams used for purposes such as generating electrical energy and diverting water to irrigate cropland. However, the Rio Grande is polluted from human activities. Its water levels have significantly declined over the past century from human activities and changes in climate. Hydrologists play an important role in collecting data that shows how much water runs through the river, how much water is used for different human activities, and what pollutants are in the water.

1. A hydrologist needs to know how much water will run off into a river after an exceptionally rainy spring. What data will the hydrologist need to consider? Choose all that apply.

   A. air temperature

   B. amount of precipitation in the winter

   C. depth of snowpack on surrounding mountain peaks

   D. stream flow rates

   E. reservoir water depth

2. Why is the work of hydrologists important?

3. What type of information about water and the water cycle would be important for a hydrologist to focus on in your community?

4. **Collaborate** Work with a small group to list the sources of drinking water in your community, such as lakes, rivers, and reservoirs. Think about why that source was chosen for use. Then consider a scenario that could reduce the amount of clean, fresh water available to the residents of the community. Together, "think like a hydrologist" to describe the scenario and to make predictions about the outcome. Create a brochure to provide to the community explaining the situation.

Can You Explain It?

Name: Date:

How could the water in a dinosaur's drink end up in a raindrop today?

EVIDENCE NOTEBOOK

Refer to the notes in your Evidence Notebook to help you construct an explanation for how some of the water molecules in a dinosaur's drink could be the very same ones in a raindrop today.

1. State your claim. Make sure your claim fully explains how the water molecules in a raindrop falling today also could have been ingested by a dinosaur millions of years ago.

2. Summarize the evidence you have gathered to support your claim and explain your reasoning.

Checkpoints

Answer the following questions to check your understanding of the lesson.

Use the photo to answer Questions 3–5.

3. What state(s) of water do you directly observe in this photo? Choose all that apply.

   A. liquid

   B. solid

   C. gas

4. As the snow forms in the atmosphere, the water molecules gain / lose / neither gain nor lose kinetic energy.

5. How will the environment shown in the photo change when summer arrives? Select all that apply.

   A. The snow will melt.

   B. The water will evaporate from the stream.

   C. Transpiration could occur.

   D. Snow will continue to fall and form large piles.

Use the photo to answer Questions 6–8.

6. Which of the following steps of the water cycle can you infer are taking place in this scene at the moment the photo was taken? Choose all that apply.

   A. evaporation

   B. sublimation

   C. condensation

   D. transpiration

7. Using numbers 1–4, order the following events in a sequence that most logically describes the movement of water from the ocean to the bottom of a well in a village on the island.

   _____ condensation

   _____ infiltration

   _____ evaporation

   _____ precipitation

8. Water in the clouds in this scene eventually moves from the atmosphere to the land by infiltration / precipitation / evaporation.

   Next, transpiration / melting / runoff carries that water to the sea.

   Wind / Gravity drives both examples of water movement.

Interactive Review

Complete this section to review the main concepts of the lesson.

The water on Earth can be found in three states: as a solid, liquid, and a gas. Changes in thermal energy cause water to change states.

A. Explain how water changes state by using an example.

Water in the atmosphere affects cloud formation and precipitation.

B. Use a sequence of at least four events to describe some of the ways that water moves into, through, and then out of the atmosphere.

Water moves on Earth's surface, below Earth's surface, and in Earth's oceans.

C. Make a table to describe at least one way that water moves in each of these parts of the Earth system: in the oceans, above ground, and below ground.

Water molecules can follow many different paths through the water cycle.

D. Explain the roles of sunlight and gravity in the water cycle.

Choose one of the activities to explore how this unit connects to other topics.

☐ People in Engineering

Kaitlin Liles, Thermal Engineer Kaitlin Liles joined NASA while a student at Virginia Tech, where she later earned a degree in mechanical engineering. Liles uses computers models and conducts real-world tests in thermal vacuum chambers. Liles served as the lead thermal engineer on NASA's Stratospheric Aerosol and Gas Experiment III. Liles helped design the instrument to withstand the extreme temperatures of space during its mission on the International Space Station.

   Research how spacecraft temperature is regulated. Create a short presentation to share your findings.

☐ Environmental Science Connection

Passive Solar Design Heating and cooling a building requires a lot of energy and can be very expensive. Buildings designed to use the sun's energy for warmth in the winter and to minimize solar heating in the summer are becoming more popular. These passive solar buildings can reduce the need for energy and reduce heating and cooling costs.

   Research the features of a passive solar building. Draw a diagram that explains how the features keep the building warm in the winter by maximizing energy transfer from the sun and cool in the summer by minimizing energy transfer from the sun.

☐ Social Studies Connection

Chilling Out People often open and close refrigerator doors a dozen or more times a day. We count on refrigerators to minimize thermal energy transfer and keep our food cold, so it stays fresh and does not spoil. Today, most of us take the refrigerator for granted, but people did not always have easy access to fresh, cold food.

   Research the history of the refrigerator. Create a timeline to show the progression from iceboxes to the modern-day refrigerator. Include key events along the way in developing this technology.

Name: _____   Date: _____

Complete this review to check your understanding of the unit.

Use the image of the fan to answer Questions 1 and 2.

1. To be more energy efficient, the fan should transform as much of the electrical energy input as possible into:

   A. kinetic energy of the fan blades

   B. sound energy in the fan's motor

   C. thermal energy in the fan's motor

   D. electromagnetic energy in the fan's blades

2. A transformation of chemical energy to electrical energy would occur if the fan were plugged into:

   A. a solar-powered generator

   B. a wind-powered generator

   C. a hydro-powered generator

   D. a fuel-powered generator

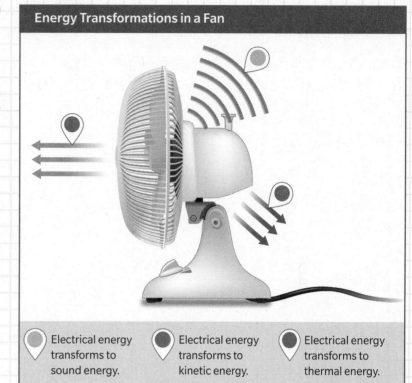

Energy Transformations in a Fan

Electrical energy transforms to sound energy.

Electrical energy transforms to kinetic energy.

Electrical energy transforms to thermal energy.

Use the photo to answer Questions 3 and 4.

3. Which processes are missing from this model of the water cycle? Select all that apply.

   A. sublimation

   B. transpiration

   C. evaporation

   D. precipitation

4. What labels would you add to this model to show how gravity drives water cycling between the Earth's surface and the atmosphere?

   A. evaporation on the surface of water

   B. precipitation falling from clouds to the water

   C. air current circulation

   D. ocean current circulation

5. Complete the table by providing examples of how each system relates to each big-picture concept.

System	Forms of energy	Transfer of energy	Transformation of energy	Scale, proportic and quantity
Roller coaster	mechanical, kinetic, potential, electrical			
Diesel engine				
River				

Name: _____   Date: _____

Use the images of the fish tank and fish bowl to answer Questions 6–9.

6. Compare the thermal energy in each container if the water is the same temperature.

7. If you start with water at the same temperature in both containers without fish and add the same amount of ice to each tank, which container would cool more quickly?

8. Assume a heater is added to each container, again starting with water at the same temperature. How would the energy required to heat the containers to a new temperature differ? Explain your reasoning.

9. Suppose identical aquarium ornaments that are the same temperature, but warmer than the water, are added to each container. If the water in each container is originally the same temperature, which piece will cool more quickly? How would the overall change in water temperature differ between the two containers over time?

Use the body temperature graph to answer Questions 10–13.

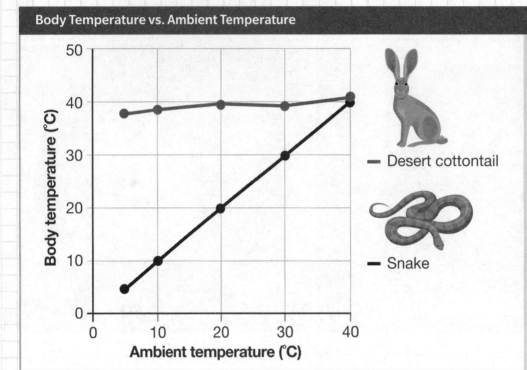

Body Temperature vs. Ambient Temperature

— Desert cottontail

— Snake

Warm-blooded animals, such as desert cottontails, tend to maintain a stable body temperature in normal environmental conditions. The body temperatures of cold-blooded animals, such as snakes, are dependent on their environment.

10. Describe the body temperatures of a desert cottontail and a snake compared to their surrounding (ambient) temperature.

11. When the snake's body temperature increases, where does the energy come from?

12. Snakes do not have an internal mechanism to regulate body temperature. How could a snake stay cool on a hot day?

13. Humans are able to maintain a nearly constant internal body temperature of about 37 °C even when it is very hot by perspiring. How does this process work to cool a person's body?

Name: _____   Date: _____

How can you cool water faster?

Hyperthermia, or heat stroke, is a life-threatening condition of elevated body temperature. Emergency medical providers know that the best way to treat people suffering from hyperthermia is to cool them very quickly by submerging them in cold water. This lifesaving process must be performed as quickly as possible to avoid deadly complications.

You are on a team of first responders tasked with developing a first aid station by the organizing committee of a local marathon. This first aid station will need to be prepared to treat runners suffering from hyperthermia. You will have large tubs of water available, along with two different forms of ice—crushed and cubed. Which type of ice should your team use to cool the tub of water as rapidly as possible? Prepare a report for the committee that includes your recommendation of which type of ice to use.

Crushed ice

Whole ice cubes

The steps below will help guide your research and recommend a solution.

Engineer It

1. **Define the Problem** What is the engineering problem you are trying to solve? Describe your criteria and constraints.

Engineer It

2. **Develop a Model** Prepare a diagram that shows how the transfer of energy occurs within the system. Describe how the problem could be modeled on a smaller scale for testing.

3. **Design an Investigation** Develop a procedure for testing the solutions to obtain measurable data. What could you use as your experimental control?

4. **Compare Solutions** Gather information from multiple sources about how to best treat hyperthermia. Consider possible biases in the sources. Describe how each type of ice would transfer thermal energy in a large water bath. What other factors might you need to consider when selecting the best solution?

5. **Identify and Recommend a Solution** Identify which type of ice to use at the first aid station, and share your recommendation with the organizing committee.

Self-Check

	I defined the engineering problem, including the criteria and constraints.
	I developed a model representing the problem.
	I designed an investigation to meaningfully compare the solutions.
	I compared the solutions based on performance and other considerations.
	I identified and recommended a solution.

Weather and Climate

How do circulation of air and water affect weather and climate in California?

Foggy summer mornings in San Francisco happen as water from the Pacific Ocean evaporates into the air and then condenses. Wind carries the foggy air over land.

You Solve It Can You Explain the Different Climate in Two California Cities? Choose two cities for parks that will showcase different organisms and climates, and use data from maps to explain why the climate is different in the two locations.

Go online and complete the You Solve It to explore ways to solve a real-world problem.

Investigate Severe Weather

Lightning can occur during thunderstorms, hurricanes, and heavy snowstorms.

A. Look at the photo. On a separate sheet of paper, write down as many different questions as you can about the photo.

B. **Discuss** With your class or a partner, share your questions. Record any additional questions generated in your discussion. Then choose the most important questions from the list that are related to severe weather. Write them below.

C. Choose a type of severe weather that you'd like to research. You will research one region affected by this type of severe weather.

D. Use the information above, along with your research, to develop a climate model and explain the causes of the severe weather you chose.

Discuss the next steps for your Unit Project with your teacher and go online to download the Unit Project Worksheet.

Language Development

Use the lessons in this unit to complete the network and expand your understanding of these key concepts.

Similar term
Phrase
Cognate
Example
Definition

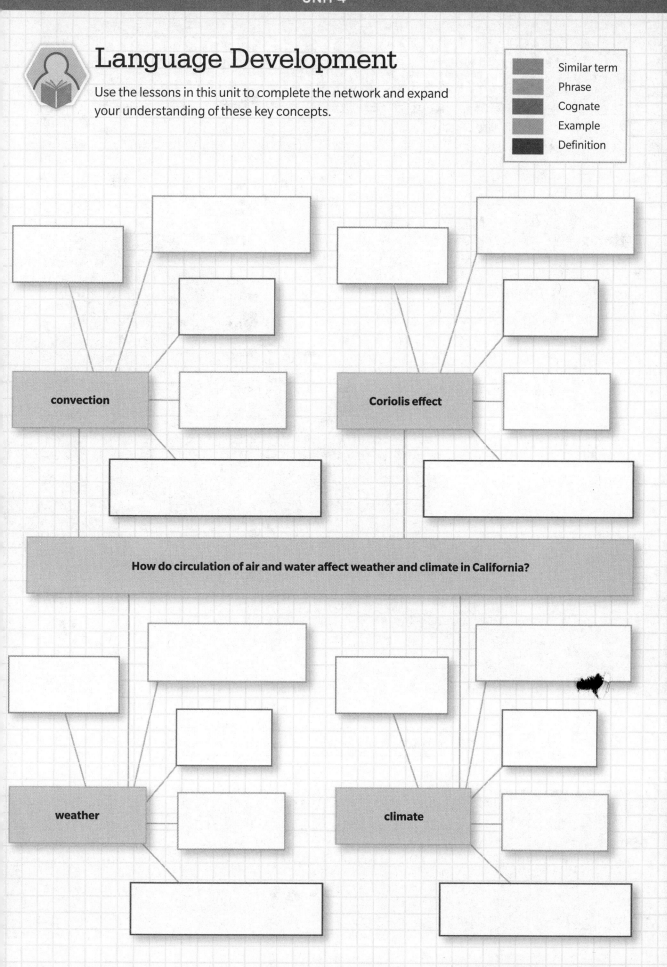

convection

Coriolis effect

How do circulation of air and water affect weather and climate in California?

weather

climate

Air Moves in Patterns in Earth's Atmosphere

Strong continual winds cause these trees to grow at an angle at the Point Reyes National Seashore in California.

Explore First

Modeling the Rate of Warming Each day, the sun warms Earth. Develop a model to explore how quickly or slowly the sun warms at least two different surfaces. How could you measure the rate of warming? How might different rates of warming cause circulation in the air nearby?

Go online to view the digital version of the Hands-On Lab for this lesson and to download additional lab resources.

CAN YOU EXPLAIN IT?

How is it possible for dust from the Sahara to end up in the Amazon?

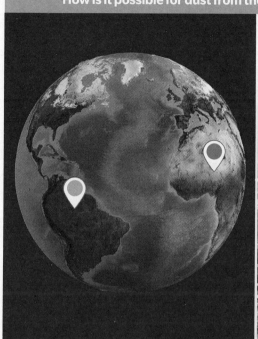

Sahara

Amazon

Scientists have discovered that about 22,000 tons of phosphorus is deposited in the Amazon every year. The strange thing is that the phosphorus comes from the Sahara! The middle of the Amazon in South America is more than 9,000 kilometers from the middle of the Sahara desert in Africa.

1. What explanation can you suggest for how dust from the Sahara can travel over 9,000 kilometers, across the ocean, and then settle in the Amazon jungle?

EVIDENCE NOTEBOOK As you explore the lesson, gather evidence to help explain how dust and other particles can travel so far.

Modeling Wind and Convection

The *atmosphere* is a mixture of gases that surrounds Earth. We often refer to this mixture of gases as *air*. Although you cannot see it, air is matter. Air moves from one place to another. We know this movement as *wind*. The atmosphere also contains small particles of liquid and solid matter, such as water droplets, ash, and ice.

2. **Discuss** The atmosphere is just one part of the larger Earth system. The Earth system also includes organisms in the biosphere, water in the hydrosphere, and rocks and minerals in the geosphere. Describe how the atmosphere interacts with other parts of the Earth system in each photo.

Winter winds in the Kronotsky Reserve, Russia

Hurricane in Baja California, Mexico

Wildfire in Santa Paula, California

Energy From the Sun and Wind

The sun emits energy that travels through space and enters the Earth system. Some of that energy can be seen as light, and some of it is invisible. Matter in the atmosphere and on Earth's surface absorbs, reflects, and transfers the sun's energy.

To understand why wind blows, you must first understand that Earth has temperature differences. Temperature differences occur because some areas receive more direct sunlight than others do. For example, the equator receives more direct sunlight than the poles, so the equator is generally warmer. Earth's temperatures also vary because some surfaces absorb more energy than others do. For example, the oceans absorb more solar energy than land does, and land absorbs more solar energy than air does. Surfaces also absorb and release energy at different rates. For example, land warms and cools faster than water does.

Hands-On Lab
Model the Formation of Wind

Use a physical model to explain how differences in air pressure form wind.

    The motions of air particles cause the particles to run into each other and into objects on Earth. The force of air particles pressing on other particles and objects is known as *air pressure*.

MATERIALS
• bottle, plastic, 1 L, with a hole punched in the side toward the bottom
• duct tape
• marshmallows, small
• pump cap that pumps air into a plastic bottle

Procedure and Analysis

STEP 1   Cover the hole in the plastic bottle with a small piece of tape. Fill the bottle $\frac{3}{4}$ full with small marshmallows. Then thread the pump cap onto the top of the bottle and tighten. The pump cap will allow you to put more air into the bottle. Do not pump it yet.

STEP 2   Look at the shape of the marshmallows. Record your observations in the table.

STEP 3   Squeeze the bottle and observe how it feels. Then shake the bottle and note what you hear. Record your observations.

STEP 4   Hold your thumb over the taped hole while your partner pumps the cap as much as he or she can. This will add more air particles into the bottle. Squeeze the bottle again, and observe the marshmallows. Record your observations.

STEP 5   Carefully shake the bottle, keeping the hole covered. Note what you hear. Record your observations.

Type of Observation	Steps 2–3	Steps 4–5
Shape of marshmallows		
Feel of bottle		
Sound when shaking bottle		

STEP 6 What differences do you observe in the bottle or its contents before air was pumped into the bottle and after?

STEP 7 Predict what might happen if you remove the tape from the hole. Before doing so, tip the bottle horizontally and shake it to distribute the marshmallows evenly over the surface. Remove the tape, and describe what happens.

prediction:

observations:

STEP 8 You pumped air into the bottle, so the air pressure in the bottle was greater than the air pressure outside the bottle. Explain how this experiment models the relationship between air pressure and the formation of wind.

The Formation of Wind

At any given time, there are air temperature differences all around Earth. As air gets warmer, it expands and its density decreases. *Density* refers to the mass per unit volume of a material. High-pressure air flows toward low-pressure air, causing wind.

In the experiment, the higher density of air particles in the bottle represented an area of high pressure. The air flowed out of the bottle because the air outside the bottle was less dense and therefore had a lower air pressure.

3. **Draw** In the diagram, the column of air on the left represents a specific volume of cold air. The same volume of warm air is shown on the right. Draw an arrow in the box to show which direction the wind would blow.

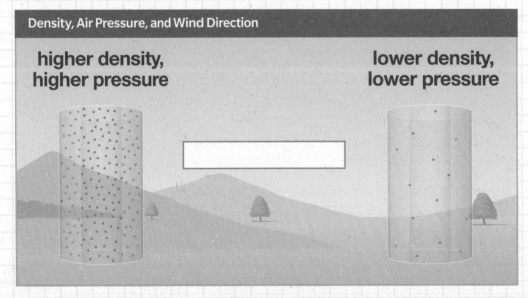

Density, Air Pressure, and Wind Direction

higher density, higher pressure

lower density, lower pressure

Convection

Cool, dense air sinks to Earth's surface and spreads out. As it spreads out, it pushes away warm, less dense air. This causes the warm air to rise. The cool air, now at the surface, begins to warm. The warm air that was pushed up begins to cool and become denser. If it becomes denser than the surrounding air, it sinks back toward the surface. This cycling of matter due to different densities is called **convection**.

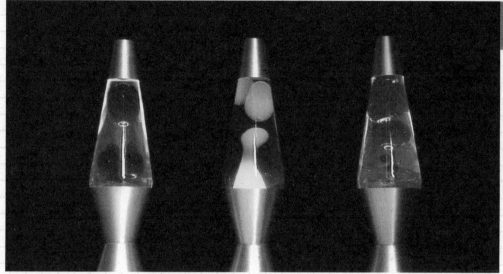

These lava lamps show convection. The colored wax at the bottom is warmed, becoming less dense. The more dense material surrounding the warm wax sinks. This pushes the wax up until it cools and becomes more dense than the surrounding material. The dense wax sinks.

4. Which statements about air in the atmosphere are true? For each statement, write T for "true" or F for "false."

_____ Warm air pushes cool air downward.

_____ Rising air cools and may become more dense than the air around it.

_____ Cool air pushes warm air upward.

_____ Air that is more dense than the air around it will sink.

5. Engineer It Modern houses have systems to control internal air temperatures in times of very cold or hot weather. In these homes, hot or cool air is pumped into the interior of the house to help keep the temperature comfortable. Based on what you know about how cool and warm air circulate in the atmosphere, what might an engineer need to consider when designing a heating/cooling system for a home in a cooler climate? How might the design differ for a house found in a warmer climate?

Convection Cells

Convection can occur on a large or small scale. Look at the air in the diagram. The air near the flame is warm and less dense than the air farther from it. The cool, denser air sinks and pushes the warm air upward. As the warm air moves upward, it loses energy to other air particles. As a result, the warm air becomes cooler and sinks. When the sinking air gets near the flame, it will become warm again. The process continues. This cyclic pattern of movement caused by density differences is called a *convection cell*. Large convection cells form in Earth's atmosphere because the sun heats Earth's surface unevenly.

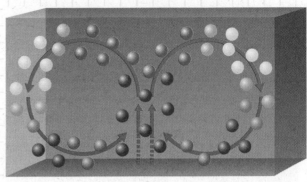

6. How does the density of air affect its movement in a convection cell?

7. **Act** Together as a group, act out the movement of air near a heat source. Assign roles to classmates, and have each participant explain what is happening to them as they move close to and away from a heat source.

Analyze Winds

Air, land, and water have different properties because they are made up of different materials. Land changes temperature more quickly than water does. Air changes temperature more quickly than either land or water. Air near the surface is warmed and cooled by being in contact with land or water at a different temperature.

8. Use the word bank to complete this paragraph and explain why the wind is blowing in the photo. You will only use some of the words in the word bank.

When the sun shines on this area, the land warms _____ than the ocean. The air above the land becomes _____ than the air above the water. The wind is blowing toward the _____ because air generally moves from cooler, high-pressure areas toward warmer, low-pressure areas.

WORD BANK
- faster
- slower
- warmer
- cooler
- land
- ocean

Explaining the Circulation of Air

Patterns of Air Circulation

Air moves in patterns in Earth's atmosphere. One reason for these patterns is the shape of Earth. Because Earth is spherical, the equator receives more energy from the sun than the north and south poles receive. This results in differences in temperature. Differences in temperature result in air pressure differences. Because air travels from high to low pressure, wind patterns result.

Earth's spin, or rotation, on its axis also affects the way that air moves across the planet's surface. The effects of Earth's rotation on the movement of air over long distances can be modeled. For example, explore the physical model shown in the photos below.

Model the Effects of Earth's Rotation on Matter in the Atmosphere

The photo at the left shows what happens to a drop of ink that is placed at the top of a stationary balloon. The photo at the right shows what happens to a drop of ink that is placed at the top of a rotating balloon. This balloon is being rotated clockwise the entire time that the ink runs down the balloon.

9. **Collaborate** With a partner, develop and use a different physical model to show how Earth's rotation affects matter in the atmosphere. Describe your model. What will you use to represent Earth? How will you model Earth's rotation? What will you use to represent matter in Earth's atmosphere? Before using your model, be sure it is approved by your teacher and you are wearing appropriate safety gear, such as gloves, goggles, and an apron.

10. **Language SmArts** Make a claim about how Earth's rotation affects matter in the atmosphere. Describe what evidence from your model supports your claim, and include a diagram or sketch.

If Earth Did Not Rotate

The sun warms the equator more than the poles. Because wind blows from cold, high-pressure areas to warm, low-pressure areas, surface winds would blow in a straight path from the poles to the equator. At the equator, the incoming cold air would push up warm air. The rising warm air would begin to cool as it flowed back toward the poles. By the time it reached the poles, it would be cold and dense enough to sink. As shown in the diagram, these motions would form two large convection cells between the equator and the poles.

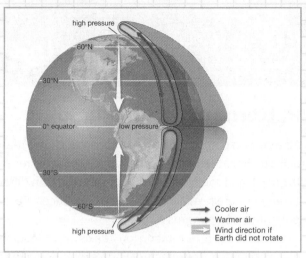

If Earth did not rotate, air would circulate in large convection cells between the poles and the equator.

The Effect of Earth's Rotation

Wind does not blow straight from the poles to the equator, because Earth is rotating. Recall the model of the rotating balloon. The ink followed a straight path when the balloon did not rotate. When the balloon rotated, the line of ink appeared to follow a curved path. Earth's rotation causes air to follow a curved path, too. Look at the white arrows on the diagram. The effect of Earth's rotation on the pathway of the wind is called the **Coriolis effect.**

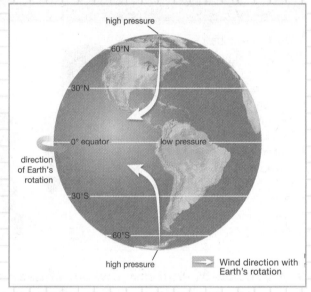

Earth's rotation causes air to deflect, or curve, away from a straight path.

The Formation of Global Wind Belts

Patterns of surface winds and convection cells change about every 30 degrees of latitude. The curving surface winds shown by the white arrows are part of the cycling air in the convection cells, shown by the red and blue arrows. Notice the bands of high and low pressure between the convection cells. Cooler, denser air sinks along bands of high pressure. Warmer, less dense air rises along bands of low pressure.

11. **Discuss** The diagram shows the result of the Coriolis effect. Compare it to the previous diagrams. Are these wind patterns what you expected? Why or why not?

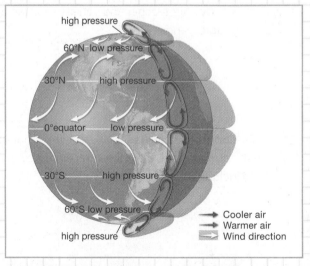

Because Earth rotates, there are global wind and pressure belts that change about every 30 degrees of latitude.

12. Use the diagram to explain how air from the equator could eventually end up in North America. How would it change temperature along the way?

Global Wind Patterns

Why does the Coriolis effect result in patterns of air flow that change every 30° of latitude? Consider the white arrows showing surface winds flowing toward the low-pressure belt at the equator. This incoming cooler air pushes up the warmer air at the equator. The warm air rises, as you can see by the arrows in the two convection cells on either side of the equator. The rising air cools and begins to travel north or south. Once it reaches about 30°N or 30°S, the air is cooler and denser than the surrounding air. The air therefore sinks along 30°N and 30°S, forming high-pressure belts along these latitudes. From there, some air travels back toward the equator and some travels toward the low-pressure belts along 60°N and 60°S.

Model of Global Winds

Global winds blow in fairly consistent, steady directions across Earth. Each global wind belt has a specific name. Global winds are also known as *prevailing winds*.

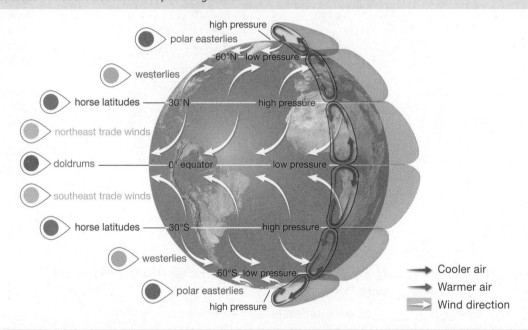

The cold *polar easterlies* blow from the northeast at the North Pole and from the southeast at the South Pole. They usually form at latitudes greater than 60°.

The *westerlies* are named for the direction from which they blow—from the west toward the east. They form between 30° and 60° latitude.

The *horse latitudes* are a narrow zone of warm, dry climates between the westerlies and the trade winds. Many deserts exist along the horse latitudes, which are found at about 30° north and south of the equator.

Warm *trade winds* blow constantly across the tropics from the east toward the west. The trade winds in the Northern Hemisphere are called the *northeast trade winds*, and those in the Southern Hemisphere are called the *southeast trade winds*. They are located between the equator and 30° latitude.

The *doldrums* are found where the trade winds of the two hemispheres meet. Winds in the doldrums are very weak, and the weather is consistently calm.

13. In what directions do prevailing winds blow in the Sahara desert, the southern Atlantic Ocean, and the Amazon? Record your evidence.

Do the Math
Compare the Hemispheres

Earth can be divided into *hemispheres*, or half spheres, in different ways. One way is to divide Earth at the equator. The Northern Hemisphere is from the equator to the North Pole, and the Southern Hemisphere is from the equator to the South Pole. Imaginary parallel lines measure north-south distances between the poles and the equator. The equator represents 0°, and the poles represent 90°N for the North Pole and 90°S for the South Pole. The distance between one of the poles and the equator is measured in 1° increments.

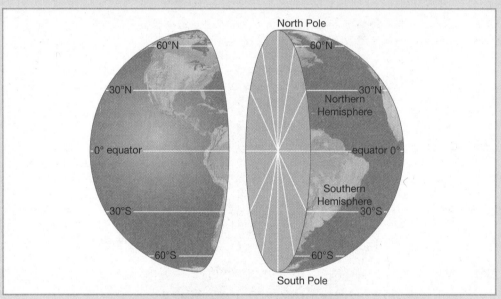

The lines of latitude are named by the angle made by a line connecting the latitude and Earth's center and a line connecting the equator and Earth's center. The location of the latitude north or south of the equator is added to the angle to indicate its relative position on the globe.

14. Fill in the blank to complete each statement correctly. Remember that *equidistant* means "the same distance."

   A. 45°N and _____ °S are equidistant from the equator.

   B. _____ °N and 78°S are equidistant from the equator.

   C. 90°N and _____ °S are equidistant from the equator.

   D. _____ °N and 15°S are equidistant from the equator.

15. The city of Boulder, Colorado, in the United States, is about 40° north of the equator, and the city of San Carlos de Bariloche, in Argentina, is about 40° south of the equator. Which statement is generally true about the wind patterns of these two cities?

   A. Their prevailing winds blow in opposite directions.

   B. Their prevailing winds blow from east to west.

   C. Their prevailing winds blow from west to east.

Relating Air Circulation to the Earth System

When it is windy outside, you can feel the air blowing against you. You feel this because air is matter. You can not see the tiny particles of air around you, but they exist and move around due to differences in temperature and density. The average, organized motion of these tiny air particles results in wind.

Wind itself is moving matter, and wind moves matter around Earth. This includes invisible matter, such as gases and microscopic bacteria. Wind also moves visible matter, such as dust, clouds, and seeds. Wind also transfers energy and affects weather patterns.

The Witch Fire destroyed over one thousand buildings and almost two-hundred thousand acres of land in San Diego County in 2007.

16. The Witch Fire occurred when dry, high-speed winds were blowing through San Diego County. These winds, called the *Santa Ana winds*, can affect Southern California in the fall and winter. The winds are warm and sometimes are even described as hot. Why might the Santa Ana winds be related to high wildfire risk?

The Cycling of Matter in the Atmosphere

Wind can pick up matter from one place and deposit it in another place. Small particles, such as the tiny water particles in clouds, can be easily moved by wind. So can lightweight matter, such as ash and feathers. Larger or heavier matter can be transported by strong winds, such as the winds generated by tornadoes and hurricanes. These movements are part of the constant cycling of matter through the Earth system.

17. **Discuss** With a partner, make a list of all of the factors that might determine how far something is carried by wind. Compare your list with other pairs' lists.

Wind can move large amounts of sediment in a short time.

Sediment, Dust, and Ash

Wind picks up dust and other sediment from the ground. Large volcanic eruptions can send ash many kilometers into the atmosphere. Global winds can spread the ash around Earth. Ash and dust in the atmosphere reflect some of the sun's incoming rays. This is why some large eruptions result in a temporary drop in the average global temperature.

Water

The atmosphere contains a lot of water. Water vapor enters the atmosphere from Earth's surface. Then, water in the atmosphere is carried by wind from one place to another, often hundreds of kilometers. Water falling from clouds in the form of precipitation soaks into soil and forms rivers and lakes. Organisms depend on this water to live. Water cycles constantly through these parts of the Earth system.

Organic Matter

The atmosphere is also part of the cycling of organic materials. For example, winds can carry pollen, seeds, bacteria, and even insects. Animals, such as birds, bats, and butterflies, depend on prevailing winds to migrate.

Carbon, Nitrogen, and Phosphorus

Other important substances that are cycled in the atmosphere are carbon, nitrogen, and phosphorus. Plants use carbon in the form of carbon dioxide during photosynthesis. You and other organisms release carbon dioxide during cellular respiration. Carbon dioxide enters the atmosphere when fossil fuels burn and when volcanoes erupt. Nitrogen is also released into the atmosphere when fossil fuels burn, during industrial processes, and when bacteria break down organic matter. Plants use nitrogen to make proteins. Animals use proteins to build body structures. Living organisms also contain the element phosphorus. As organisms excrete waste or die and decompose, phosphorous is released into soil and water. Water and wind can help cycle phosphorous through the Earth system.

EVIDENCE NOTEBOOK

18. How might the cycling of matter in Earth's atmosphere relate to dust traveling from the Sahara to the Amazon? Record your evidence.

The Flow of Energy in the Atmosphere

Matter is not the only thing that flows through Earth's atmosphere. Energy also flows through Earth's atmosphere and into, through, and out of Earth's subsystems.

The Transfer of Thermal Energy

The temperature of air is related to the random, disorganized motion of its particles. Air particles move more when air is hot and less when air is cold. *Thermal energy* is the energy something has due to the motion of its particles. A hot object has more thermal energy than a cold object does. As warm air cools, its thermal energy decreases.

The sun's energy travels in waves through space in a process called *radiation*. When the sun's energy is absorbed by Earth's surface, the surface becomes warmer than the air above it. The surface's thermal energy increases. When air particles and surface particles touch, thermal energy is transferred from the warmer surface particles to the cooler air particles. The energy transfer that happens when particles touch is called *conduction*. As air warms, its particles move farther apart. The air becomes less dense. The warmer, less dense air may rise if cooler, denser air flows in and pushes up the warm air. The flow of air due to differences in density is an example of convection. *Convection* is the transfer of energy due to the movement of matter.

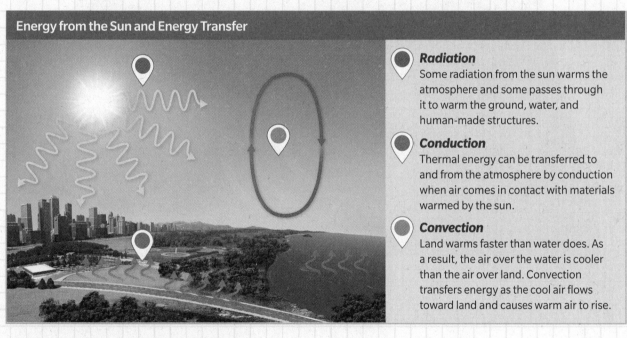

Energy from the Sun and Energy Transfer

Radiation
Some radiation from the sun warms the atmosphere and some passes through it to warm the ground, water, and human-made structures.

Conduction
Thermal energy can be transferred to and from the atmosphere by conduction when air comes in contact with materials warmed by the sun.

Convection
Land warms faster than water does. As a result, the air over the water is cooler than the air over land. Convection transfers energy as the cool air flows toward land and causes warm air to rise.

The Transfer of Kinetic Energy

In addition to transfers of thermal energy in the Earth system, there are transfers of kinetic energy. *Kinetic energy* is the energy of motion. For example, the kinetic energy of wind is transferred to ocean water as wind forms waves. Waves help drive ocean surface currents. The kinetic energy of the wind also moves solid material, such as the sand in deserts. Therefore, over time, wind can shape Earth's surface.

19. How might the transfer of thermal energy and of kinetic energy by wind affect water molecules on Earth's surface and in the atmosphere?

Case Study: The Santa Ana Winds

The Santa Ana winds are dry, warm winds that can blow at high-speeds through Southern California during the fall and winter. The winds can form when there is an area of cold, high-pressure air around the Great Basin, and an area of warm, low-pressure air near Southern California. The high-pressure air travels quickly toward the low-pressure air. Elevation decreases along the way, causing the winds to become drier. Wind speeds increase as the air travels through narrow canyons and valleys. The Santa Ana winds eventually reach Southern California, where they can damage trees and structures, dry out vegetation, and worsen the effects of wildfires.

Formation of the Santa Ana Winds

A cold mass of high-pressure air can form over the Great Basin during the fall and winter. If there is an area of low-pressure air off the coast of Southern California at the same time, the Santa Ana winds form, following the route shown by the arrows in this diagram.

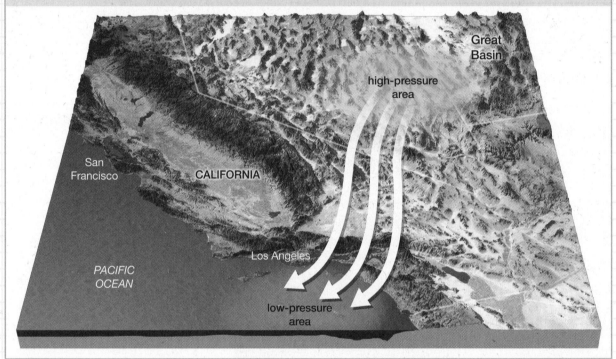

Explain the Santa Ana Winds

20. The atmosphere is interacting with the geosphere / hydrosphere as the Santa Ana Winds flow through canyons and valleys. These winds can cause fires to spread and burn vegetation in the geosphere / biosphere.

21. **Language SmArts** Think again about the Witch Fire in San Diego county. Explain how the Santa Ana winds can worsen the effects of wildfires like the Witch Fire. Use evidence from the diagram and the text to support your explanation.

_____

_____

_____

_____

_____

Continue Your Exploration

Name: _____ Date: _____

Check out the path below or go online to choose one of the other paths shown.

Jet Streams

- **People in Science**
- **Farming for Energy**
- **Hands-On Labs** ✋
- **Propose Your Own Path**

Go online to choose one of these other paths.

A *jet stream* is a narrow belt of fast-moving wind that forms several kilometers high in the atmosphere. Jet streams flow from west to east because of Earth's rotation. They travel at least 92 kilometers per hour (km/h) and sometimes up to 450 km/h.

Jet streams flow above the boundaries between warm and cool air. The greater the temperature difference between the bodies of air, the faster the jet stream will travel. Temperature differences are usually greater in the winter, so jet streams are strongest during this season. The locations of jet streams are also affected by the position of the sun during different seasons. For example, in the summer in the Northern Hemisphere, the temperature boundaries are farther north, so the jet stream is farther north. In the winter, the cold air moves farther south, so the jet stream is farther south.

Jet streams are above the surface winds you can feel near the ground. Even though jet streams do not flow along Earth's surface, they do affect you. Jet streams influence weather patterns. In the diagram you can see some of Earth's major jet streams.

1. Jet streams flow several kilometers above the surface where airplanes can fly. Therefore, the length of an airplane trip could be affected if the airplane traveled along a jet stream. For example, an airplane trip from Las Vegas to Orlando would be faster / slower than a trip from Orlando to Las Vegas if the jet stream moved over these cities.

Jet Streams

Both the Northern Hemisphere and the Southern Hemisphere have two main kinds of jet streams. The polar jet stream travels between 50° to 60° north or south of the equator. The subtropical jet stream is closer to the equator.

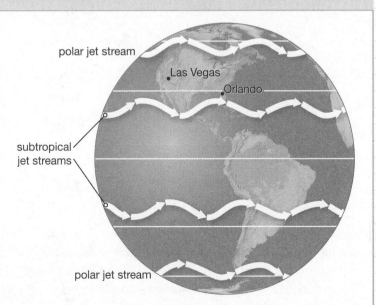

polar jet stream

Las Vegas

Orlando

subtropical jet streams

polar jet stream

Continue Your Exploration

2. Use evidence from the diagram to explain why the airplane trip is faster one way.

3. Would this airplane trip always be faster one way? Explain why or why not.

4. Explain why no jet stream exists at the equator.

5. **Collaborate** Do research to find out how jet streams affect weather patterns where you live. Compare your findings with a partner to plan and deliver an oral presentation to your class. Use multimedia and visuals from your research to explain how jet streams influence your local weather.

Can You Explain It?

Name: **Date:**

How is it possible for dust from the Sahara to end up in the Amazon?

Sahara

Amazon

EVIDENCE NOTEBOOK

Refer to the notes in your Evidence Notebook to help you construct an explanation as to how it is possible for dust from the Sahara to end up in the Amazon.

1. State your claim. Make sure your claim fully explains how material from the Sahara ended up in the Amazon.

2. Summarize the evidence you have gathered to support your claim and explain your reasoning.

Checkpoints

Answer the following questions to check your understanding of the lesson.

Use the illustration to answer Questions 3–5.

3. Which of the following is a characteristic of all global winds?

   A. They all move from areas of high pressure to areas of low pressure.

   B. They all move from areas of low pressure to areas of high pressure.

   C. They all move in the same direction toward the equator.

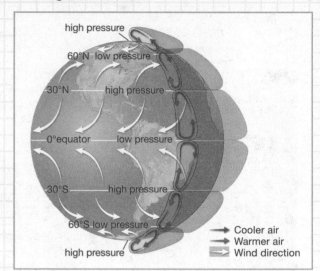

4. Which factors have the greatest impact on the direction of global winds? Choose one.

   A. air speed and the amount of daylight

   B. rotation of Earth and pressure differences

   C. length of the day and temperature of the air

   D. distance from the horse latitudes and size of the sun

5. Many dry desert climates are found around 30° N and 30° S latitude. Which factor has the most influence on the formation of desert climates?

   A. dry air rising at 30° latitudes

   B. dry air descending at 30° latitudes

   C. low amounts of rainfall at other latitudes

   D. high rates of evaporation at the equator

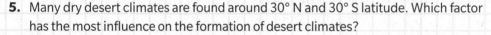

Use the illustration to answer Questions 6 and 7.

6. The sun warms the dark-colored road faster than the surrounding fields. Order the statements from 1–4 to describe what happens next.

   _____ The warm air above the road rises and loses energy as it cools.

   _____ The air above the road becomes warmer and less dense than the air above the fields.

   _____ The denser, cooler air over the fields sinks and flows toward the road.

   _____ The denser, cooler air sinks back down to Earth's surface.

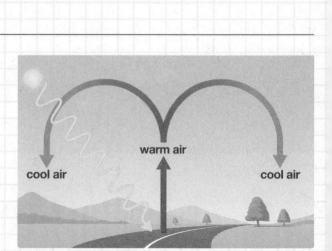

7. The red and blue arrows in the diagram represent the transfer of thermal energy by the process of *conduction / convection / radiation*.

Interactive Review

Complete this section to review the main concepts of the lesson.

Wind forms when air moves from an area of high pressure to an area of low pressure.

A. Draw a convection cell and label the source of thermal energy, the air temperature and density, and the directions of air flow.

The unequal heating of Earth's surface by the sun and deflection caused by the Coriolis effect cause distinct patterns of global winds.

B. On a large scale, what causes winds to move east and west in patterns across Earth's surface?

Circulation in Earth's atmosphere moves air around the planet and plays a role in the cycling of matter and the flow of energy in the Earth system.

C. How does wind transfer thermal and kinetic energy?

Water Moves in Patterns in Earth's Oceans

Scientists used satellite data to construct this map of ocean surface currents. Red and yellow represent faster currents. Green and blue represent slower currents.

Explore First

Determining Density When an object is less dense than water, it will float, but if the object is more dense, it will sink. Fill one plastic tub with salty water, and one with fresh water. Test five different objects to see if they sink or float in each tub. Does water's salinity affect whether each object sinks or floats? What is the relationship between the salinity and density of water?

Go online to view the digital version of the Hands-On Lab for this lesson and to download additional lab resources.

CAN YOU EXPLAIN IT?

Why does floating garbage tend to build up in certain places in the ocean?

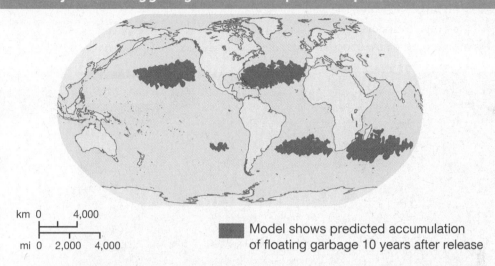

km 0   4,000

mi 0   2,000   4,000

■ Model shows predicted accumulation of floating garbage 10 years after release

Have you ever wondered what happens when someone throws trash such as a plastic bottle into the ocean? This map shows where floating garbage is likely to collect. The purple areas show where floating garbage is most likely to be found ten years after it is dumped into the ocean.

1. What explanation can you suggest for how floating garbage could be moved around in the ocean?

2. What might cause floating objects to collect in one area in a body of water?

 EVIDENCE NOTEBOOK As you explore the lesson, gather evidence to help explain how floating garbage could build up in certain areas of the ocean.

Modeling Surface Currents

Patterns in the Ocean

Using satellite data about ocean water, the National Aeronautics and Space Administration (NASA) made models of water movements on the ocean surface. The white lines in the map show the flow of ocean water in October 2005.

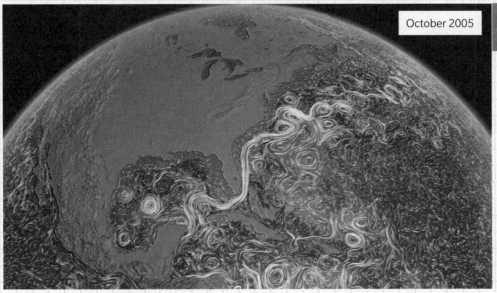

October 2005

Explore Online

3. What patterns do you see in the movement of the ocean surface?

4. Why do you think there is so much movement in the ocean?

The Formation of Surface Currents

When you look out over the ocean, you might see floating objects being carried along by the movement of water. Although it may be hard to see ocean water moving, it flows in regular patterns. The streamlike movement of ocean water in a regular pattern is called an **ocean current.** As you can see in the map, some ocean currents flow at or near the ocean's surface. This horizontal movement of water in a regular pattern at the ocean's surface is called a *surface current*.

Surface Winds

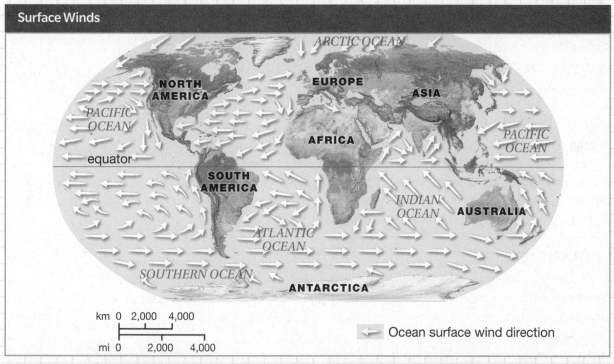

km 0 2,000 4,000

mi 0 2,000 4,000

⬅ Ocean surface wind direction

Surface Currents

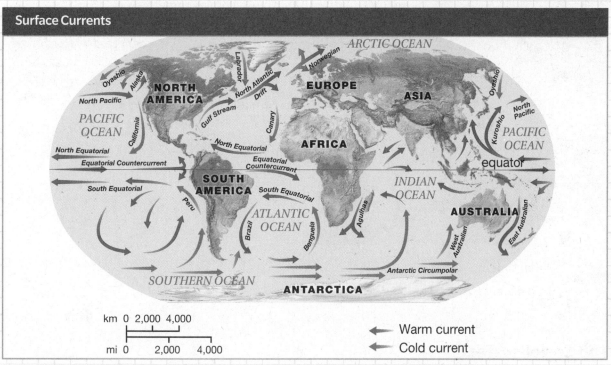

km 0 2,000 4,000

mi 0 2,000 4,000

⬅ Warm current

⬅ Cold current

5. What patterns do you see when comparing the global surface winds with the global surface currents in these maps?

A. In most areas, the winds and the currents move in opposite directions.

B. In most areas, the winds and the currents move in similar directions.

6. More of the sun's energy is received near the equator than near the poles. This uneven warming causes _____ differences in the atmosphere. The pressure differences cause _____. As wind blows, energy is transferred from the wind to the ocean. The energy transfer causes the water to move in surface ocean _____.

WORD BANK
• currents
• pressure
• wind

Factors That Affect Surface Currents

Surface currents in Earth's oceans are influenced by three factors: global winds, the locations of the continents, and Earth's rotation, which causes the Coriolis effect. These factors keep surface currents flowing in distinct patterns around Earth.

Global Winds

Surface winds cause surface currents by transferring kinetic energy to ocean water. Think about what happens if you blow across the surface of a liquid in a cup. The transfer of energy from your breath to the liquid causes liquid to move across the cup. In a similar way, winds that blow across the oceans cause ocean water to move, forming surface currents. The currents generally flow in the same direction as the winds.

Continents

As you can see in the map, when surface currents reach continents, the currents change direction. *Continental deflection* refers to the change in the direction of currents as they meet continents. For example, when the Peru Current reaches the coast of South America, it is deflected toward the west.

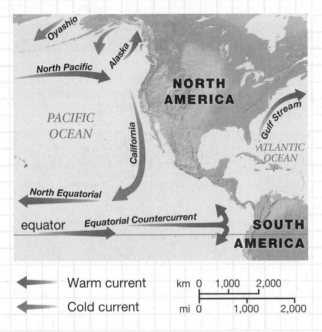

Warm current
Cold current

km 0   1,000   2,000
mi 0   1,000   2,000

7. The California Current travels south / north / west from where the North Pacific Current is deflected by North America. The California current eventually turns toward the south / north / west and joins the North Equatorial Current.

The Coriolis Effect

Earth's surface currents flow in huge circular patterns, called *gyres* (JYRZ). One reason for this circular flow is the rotation of Earth on its axis. Earth's circumference at the equator is larger than its circumference near the poles. So, points near the equator travel faster than points closer to the poles travel. As matter, such as a mass of air, moves from a pole toward the equator, the matter moves more slowly than the ground beneath it does. As a result, winds and water traveling south from the North Pole deflect in a clockwise direction to the right. And winds and water traveling from the South Pole deflect in a counterclockwise direction to the left. This deflection of moving objects from a straight path as a result of Earth's rotation is called the *Coriolis effect*. The Coriolis effect is only noticeable for objects that travel over long distances, such as Earth's wind and water. The Coriolis effect causes water to drift inward a bit toward the center of the gyres.

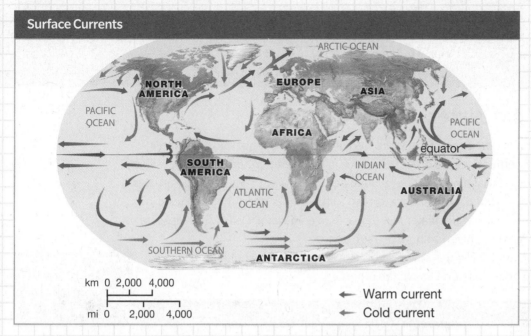

Surface Currents

km 0 2,000 4,000

mi 0 2,000 4,000

← Warm current

← Cold current

8. What do you notice on the map about the pattern of the gyres in the Northern Hemisphere as compared to the gyres in the Southern Hemisphere?

EVIDENCE NOTEBOOK

9. Think about how ocean surface currents could affect floating garbage. Record your evidence.

Explain Sea Surface Temperatures

Scientists use infrared and microwave sensors to gather sea surface temperature data. From these data, they make color-enhanced maps that help them study ocean surface currents.

10. The sea surface temperature at the point labeled *east* is _____. The sea surface temperature at the point labeled *west* is _____.

11. The points *east* and *west* are at the same latitude, so they receive about the same amount of solar energy. Explain why points *east* and *west* have different ocean temperatures.

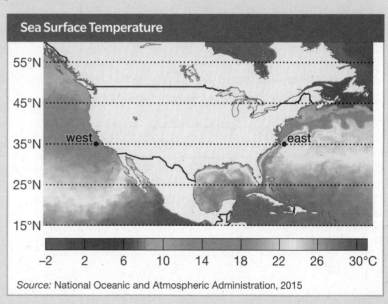

Sea Surface Temperature

55°N

45°N

35°N   west   east

25°N

15°N

−2 2 6 10 14 18 22 26 30°C

Source: National Oceanic and Atmospheric Administration, 2015

Modeling Deep Currents

Hot and Cold Water

Hot and cold water are made up of the same kind of particles. But hot and cold water have different properties because of the difference in their temperatures. Cold water has slow-moving particles that have less energy than particles in warm water have. Particles in warm water move around more and are spread a little farther apart than particles in cold water are. This makes warm water less dense than cold water. *Density* is a measure of the amount of mass in a given volume of a substance.

What do you think will happen when cold water and warm water are put in contact with each other, with one above the other?

Explore Online

Before	After
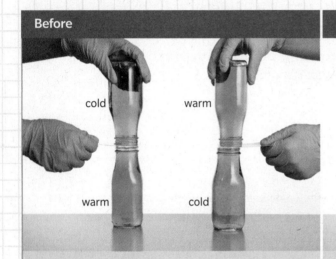	
The blue water is cold. The red water is warm. Bottles of water at different temperatures are placed on top of each other with a plastic card separating the warm water from the cold. The plastic cards are removed from between the bottles. The cold and warm water come into contact.	This shows the same bottles a few minutes after the plastic cards were removed.

12. Use the table to record your observations of what happened in each pair of bottles. Then write an explanation for your observations.

Experiment	Observations	Possible Explanation
cold warm		
warm cold		

Hands-On Lab
Explore Density Differences in Water

Design and carry out an investigation to see why sometimes water moves relative to water nearby, and sometimes it does not. Test water at different temperatures and salinities. *Salinity* is a measure of the amount of salt in water.

Density can be measured in the units of kilograms per meter cubed (kg/m^3). Fresh water has a density of about 1000 kg/m^3. Density can be used to predict whether items will float or sink in water. For example, if a piece of metal has a greater density than that of water, the metal will sink in water. In gases and liquids, matter that is more dense than the matter that surrounds it will sink toward Earth's center.

Food coloring was added to the water in these bags.

Procedure and Analysis

STEP 1 Look at the photo. You can test how differences in temperature and salinity affect water's movement by putting your water samples in a zipper bag. Seal the bag so that there are no bubbles left in the bag. It is okay if a little water spills out of the bag as you are sealing it. Then gently place the bag in a large container of water and see where your bag comes to rest.

STEP 2 Write a plan for investigating the relationships of temperature and salinity to the density of water.

STEP 3 On a separate sheet of paper, design a table like the sample table shown or use another method to record data from your investigation.

Sample	Water Temperature	Amount of Salt Added	Results

STEP 4 Carry out your investigation and collect data.

STEP 5 What patterns do you see in your results?

STEP 6 Use what you learned in this activity to draw conclusions about the effects of temperature and salinity on the density of ocean water. State your conclusions. Summarize your evidence and explain your reasoning.

STEP 7 How might your conclusions relate to the movement of ocean water?

The Density of Ocean Water

Ocean water is not all the same. The density of ocean water changes when its temperature or salinity changes. Differences in density affect how ocean water circulates. Denser ocean water sinks and pushes up less dense water.

If you have ever accidentally swallowed some ocean water, you would say it is pretty salty. One way to express this saltiness, or salinity, is the number of grams of salt dissolved in one liter of water, or g/L. The average salinity of all the oceans is about 35 g/L, but ocean water has a range of salinities. The higher the salinity of ocean water is, the more dense it is.

The temperature of ocean water varies as well. The colder the ocean water is, the more dense it is. In polar regions, ocean temperature near the surface can be as cold as −1.9 °C. Near the equator, water temperature near the surface can be as high as 30 °C.

Do the Math
Analyze Water Density Data

Analyzing data in graphs can help you see patterns and discover relationships between variables. In each of the graphs below, one variable is held constant so that you can investigate the relationship between two other variables.

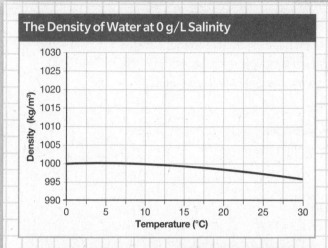

This graph shows how the density of fresh water changes as its temperature changes.

13. Water at a temperature of 10 °C has a density of about _____.

14. Water at a temperature of 25 °C has a higher / lower density than water at 10 °C does. As the temperature increases from 15 °C to 30 °C, the density of water decreases / increases.

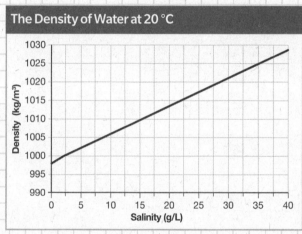

This graph shows how the density of water at 20 °C changes as its salinity changes.

15. Water with a salinity of 20 g/L has a density of _____.

16. Water with a salinity of 34 g/L has a higher / lower density than water with a salinity of 20 g/L does. As the salinity increases from 0 g/L to 40 g/L, the density of water decreases / increases.

Changes in Temperature

Temperature changes happen when ocean water absorbs or releases energy. The sun warms ocean water near the surface. When air above the ocean is at a different temperature than the water, energy is transferred and temperature changes result. Ocean water also changes temperature where ice melts and rivers flow into the ocean.

Changes in Salinity

The salinity of ocean water changes when fresh water is added or removed. For example, when rain falls into the ocean, fresh water is added, and the water's salinity decreases. During evaporation, liquid water changes to water vapor that enters the air, but dissolved particles, such as salts, remain behind. Ocean water's salinity increases during evaporation. When ocean water freezes, dissolved particles are left in the liquid part of the water, and the water's salinity increases.

17. When rivers flow into the ocean, the salinity of the ocean water
increases / decreases because the river adds *salt / fresh* water.

In an area of the ocean where a lot of evaporation but little precipitation happens, the salinity of the water is likely to *increase / decrease*. Therefore, the density is likely to *increase / decrease*.

The Formation of Deep Currents

The density of ocean water will increase if the water becomes colder or if the salinity increases. If this happens, ocean water at the surface can become denser than the water around or below it. The denser water sinks. This downward movement takes surface water into the deep ocean. *Deep ocean currents* are the movement of water in regular patterns below the surface of the ocean.

18. The diagram shows the circulation of water in a deep ocean current. Write the labels provided in the proper places on the diagram to explain the model.

- *a surface current flows toward the pole*
- *water sinks and forms a deep current*

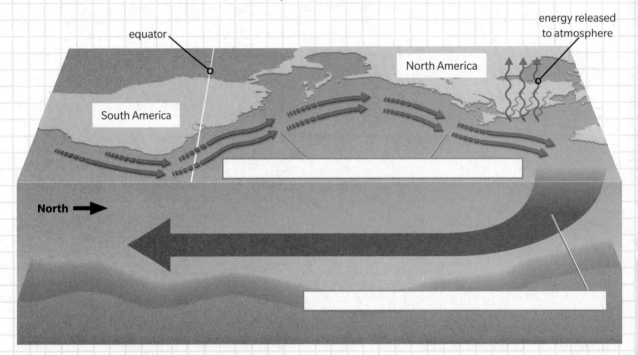

Factors that Affect Deep Currents

Deep currents are driven by density differences in ocean water and by gravity. At Earth's poles, surface water cools and becomes denser. The denser water is pulled toward the ocean floor by gravity more strongly than less dense water is. The denser water sinks and moves below the surface toward the equator, forming a deep current.

Deep currents flow along the ocean floor or along the top of another layer of water. As a result, several layers of deep currents can occur at any place in the ocean. Continents and the bottom topography of the ocean affect the path of deep ocean currents because deep currents are deflected whenever they flow toward land. And the Coriolis effect causes deep ocean currents to be deflected in the same way that surface currents are deflected.

19. **Engineer It** A water heater is a tank in which cold water is heated. Cold water flows into the tank to keep it full. A heating element warms the water inside the tank. The heated water can then be sent to hot water faucets in a building. Assume that a water heater design requires the hottest water possible to be sent to hot water faucets in a building. Where would be the best place for the hot water outlet pipe to be attached to the tank: the top, the middle, or the bottom of the tank? Explain your answer.

Analyze Currents in the Mediterranean Sea

Long ago, people observed water flowing into the Mediterranean Sea from the surface of the Atlantic Ocean, from the Black Sea, and from rivers. They noticed something very puzzling. No matter how much water flowed into the Mediterranean, its sea level remained the same. Some evaporation was occurring, but it was not enough to remove the amount of water that was entering the Mediterranean Sea.

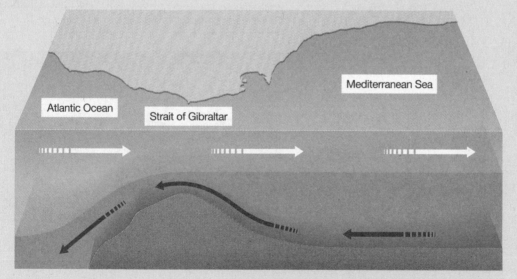

20. What processes in the Mediterranean Sea might explain why the water level of the Mediterranean did not increase, even though all the surface currents were flowing into that sea? The map and diagram may help you develop your explanation.

_____

_____

_____

_____

Relating Ocean Circulation to the Flow of Matter and Energy

The Earth system has four main subsystems. These subsystems interact in a complex and always-changing whole that we can think of as the *Earth system.* Earth's subsystems include

- the geosphere, which is the part of Earth that contains rocks, minerals, and sediment
- the biosphere, which is living things and the areas of Earth where they are found
- the atmosphere, which is the layer of air surrounding Earth
- the hydrosphere, which is all of Earth's water, including rivers, oceans, clouds, and precipitation

Oceans make up a large part of the hydrosphere because 97% of Earth's water is salt water.

21. Explain how Earth's subsystems are interacting in each photo.

A.

B.

C.

This kelp forest in the Channel Islands National Park in California provides a habitat for sea lions and other animals.

Deltas are places where rivers deposit sediment in the ocean. Some marine organisms depend on this sediment.

Ocean water evaporates, rises into the air, and then condenses. These processes can result in clouds and rain.

Convection Currents in the Ocean

The movement of matter due to differences in density is called *convection.* When denser material sinks, less dense material around it is pushed up. Convection also describes the transfer of energy due to the flow of matter. Convection can happen in gases, in liquids, and in solids that flow slowly. In the Earth system, convection happens in the atmosphere, in the ocean and other bodies of water, and in rock deep inside Earth. A convection current forms when convection happens repeatedly or in a cycle.

22. Add the following labels in the correct spaces below to complete
this general model of a convection current in the ocean:
- *deep current moves toward equator*
- *surface current moves toward pole*

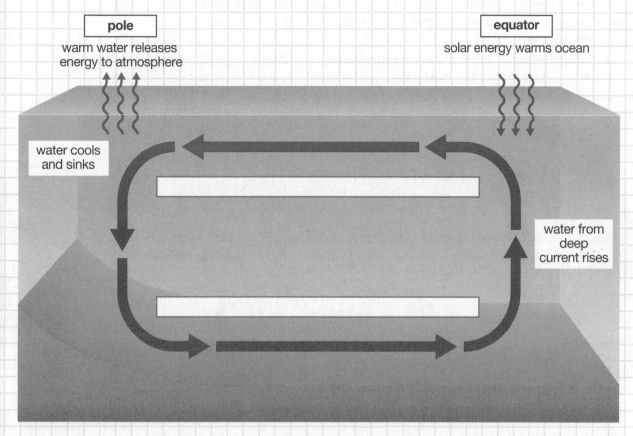

pole

warm water releases
energy to atmosphere

equator

solar energy warms ocean

water cools
and sinks

water from
deep
current rises

Convection currents involve the sinking of dense water and the rising of less dense water
in a cycle. This process takes place all over Earth's oceans to form global circulation
patterns. These patterns include surface currents that carry warm, less dense water
away from the equator toward the poles. Water from the deep ocean near the equator
rises to replace the water that is moving away on the surface. The patterns also include
deep ocean currents that carry cool, denser water away from the poles toward the
equator. These global circulation patterns affect the flow of energy and the cycling of
matter in the Earth system.

23. Language SmArts Using what you have read and observed in the diagram,
describe the path of a molecule of water in a convection current in the ocean.
Include a description of the transfers and transformations of energy that would
occur as the molecule travels in the convection current.

Global Ocean Circulation

When you put all of Earth's ocean currents together on a map or globe, you can see a pattern of water movement in the ocean. The model can be thought of as the main highway on which ocean water flows. If you could follow a molecule of water on one possible path, you might find that the molecule takes more than 1,000 years to return to its starting point!

   The model below shows an overall pattern of currents. It does not include all ocean currents. The flow of all of Earth's ocean currents is more complex than what is shown in this model and includes all of the surface currents, deep currents, and gyres.

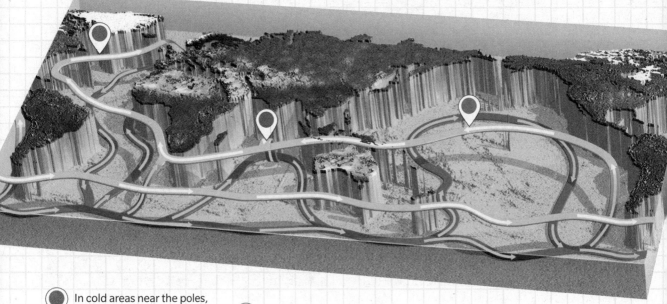

In cold areas near the poles, energy flows from the ocean into the atmosphere. The ocean water gets colder and more dense. This cooler, denser water sinks and then moves toward the equator along the ocean bottom.

In areas such as the Indian Ocean and the west coast of South America, deep water comes up to the surface. This upwelling of deep water brings cold, nutrient-rich water to the surface.

Near the equator, surface ocean water absorbs solar energy and gets warmer. This warm water tends to flow toward the poles and replace the cold water that is sinking there.

24. **Collaborate** In your school or community, there may be patterns of circulation that you can observe as groups of people move around during different times of the day. Work with a team to model these patterns with a map or drawing. Discuss with your team how the patterns you observe are like global ocean circulation and how they are different.

The Flow of Energy

The sun's energy enters Earth by the process of *radiation*. As the sun warms Earth's surface, solar energy is transformed into thermal energy. Weather and climate are affected as energy flows through the Earth system.

Energy is transferred from warmer to cooler objects. For example, when ocean water is warmer than the air above it, thermal energy flows from the water to the air by *conduction*. This process warms the air. Thermal energy is also transferred from warmer to cooler ocean water by conduction.

Energy is transferred from the equator toward the poles by *convection* as ocean water circulates around the globe. For example, cold and dense ocean water near the poles flows toward warmer, less-dense water near the equator. Warm water travels away from the equator and back toward the poles.

25. The greater the temperature difference between objects, the more quickly energy is transferred. In which location would energy be transferred more quickly?

   A. a lake at 5 °C where the air is 10 °C

   B. a lake at 2 °C where the air is 10 °C

   C. a lake at 2 °C where the air is 2 °C

26. Discuss Share your explanation with a partner. Together, determine whether energy is flowing from the air to the water or from the water to the air. Cite evidence for your explanations.

The Cycling of Matter

Ocean currents transport not only energy but also matter in the Earth system. This matter includes the ocean water itself, dissolved solids such as salt, and gases such as oxygen and carbon dioxide. Matter transported by ocean currents also includes marine organisms such as plankton. Some matter transported by ocean currents is harmful to the environment. Human waste, garbage, and other pollutants affect the environment everywhere that ocean currents carry these materials.

The cycling of matter in the Earth system also involves the chemical reactions and processes that take place in the ocean. For example, gases such as oxygen and carbon dioxide move back and forth between the ocean and the air depending on temperature, concentration of the gases, and other factors. Some marine organisms use carbon dioxide during the process of photosynthesis. During this process, organisms release oxygen into the water. The oxygen is then used by most living organisms during cellular respiration.

Diatoms are one type of plankton.

EVIDENCE NOTEBOOK

27. How might the cycling of matter in the ocean be related to the buildup of floating garbage in certain parts of the ocean? Why might some garbage float and not sink? Record your evidence.

The Carbon Cycle

This diagram shows the cycling of carbon through the Earth system, in living and nonliving subsystems. The ocean plays an important role in the carbon cycle.

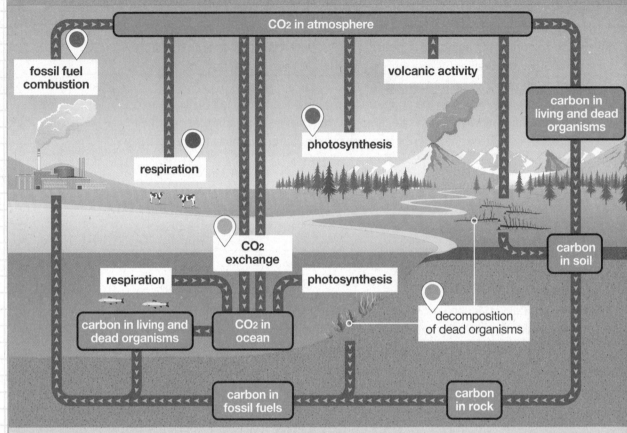

Respiration During cellular respiration, organisms take in oxygen (O_2) and release CO_2. Aquatic organisms release CO_2 into the water. Organisms on land release CO_2 into the atmosphere.

CO_2 exchange Ocean water can absorb carbon dioxide (CO_2). And CO_2 can be released from water into the air. So, the ocean plays an important role in regulating the amount of CO_2 in the air.

Photosynthesis Plants and algae use CO_2 in photosynthesis. The carbon in CO_2 is used to make sugars that are energy sources for the organisms and for the organisms that eat them.

Combustion of fossil fuels Fossil fuels contain carbon that originally came from the remains of dead plants and animals. When fossil fuels are burned, CO_2 is released into the atmosphere.

Decomposition As organisms die and decompose, carbon from their bodies goes back into the environment. This carbon may be used by other organisms, go into the soil or ocean, or form rock.

Predict Effects of a Change in Ocean Circulation

28. Describe at least two effects on the Earth system that might happen if ocean circulation stopped. Explain your reasoning.

_____

_____

_____

_____

_____

_____

Continue Your Exploration

Name: _____   Date: _____

Check out the path below or go online to choose one of the other paths shown.

Careers in Science

- Upwelling in Earth's Oceans
- Hands-On Labs ✋
- Propose Your Own Path

Go online to choose one of these other paths.

Physical Oceanographer

Oceanographers are scientists who study the ocean. There are many areas to study in oceanography. Some of these are marine ecosystems, ocean circulation, the geology of the sea floor, and the chemical and physical properties of ocean water. These topics are related. So, it is important that oceanographers have an understanding of biology, chemistry, geology, and physics to unravel the mysteries of the ocean. All oceanographers must have a four-year college degree. Most go on to earn a master's degree and a doctorate before becoming ocean scientists.

One type of oceanographer, a physical oceanographer, studies the physical conditions and processes in the ocean. This involves studying phenomena such as waves, currents, and tides; the transport of sand on and off beaches; coastal erosion; and the interactions of the atmosphere and the ocean. Physical oceanographers also study the relationships that influence weather and climate, the behavior of light and sound in water, and the ocean's interactions with the sea floor.

1. Why is it important for physical oceanographers to have studied several different fields of science?

Oceanographers work outside *Alvin*, one of the world's first deep-sea submersibles. *Alvin* can take scientists as far as 4,500 meters below the ocean surface.

A physical oceanographer brings a CTD instrument onto a research ship. The CTD takes many measurements of conductivity, temperature, and depth.

Continue Your Exploration

2. Which descriptions identify areas of science that a physical oceanographer might need to use to answer questions about the topic listed? Choose all that apply.

   A. chemistry and physics to study how currents and salinity are related

   B. physics and geology to study the transport of sand on and off beaches

   C. biology, chemistry, geology, and physics to study the interactions of the atmosphere and the ocean

3. Write at least three questions that you could investigate if you were a physical oceanographer.

4. **Engineer It** Today physical oceanographers can measure the speed of ocean currents with advanced technology. For example, floating buoys that have Global Positioning System (GPS) devices can be used to collect data about where the buoy is traveling and how fast it is going. These data can be used to calculate the speed of a current and to map its direction. Before computers and GPS devices, scientists managed to map and measure currents with fair accuracy. Propose one way you could measure the speed of a surface ocean current if you had a boat you could anchor, pieces of wood, string or rope, and a stopwatch.

5. **Collaborate** Research opposing claims about the causes of ocean acidification. Choose one claim and write an argument to support it. Be sure to use credible sources. Describe the claim, explain the evidence and reasoning behind the claim, and provide a concluding statement to support your argument.

Can You Explain It?

Name: _____ **Date:** _____

Why does floating garbage tend to build up in certain places in the ocean?

Model shows predicted accumulation of floating garbage 10 years after release

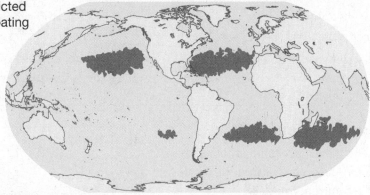

Credit: Adapted from "Origin, dynamics and evolution of ocean garbage patches from observed surface drifters, Figure 1 (c) Tracer accumulation factor after 10 years, doi:10.1088/1748-9326/7/4/044040" from Environmental Research Letters, Volume 7 by Erik van Sebille et. al. Copyright © 2012 IOP Publishing Ltd. CC BY-NC-SA. Adapted and reproduced by permission of Erik van Sebille and IOP Publishing Ltd.

EVIDENCE NOTEBOOK

Refer to the notes in your Evidence Notebook to help you construct an explanation for why floating garbage that comes mostly from the land tends to build up in certain places in the ocean.

1. State your claim. Make sure your claim fully explains how and why floating garbage builds up in certain areas.

2. Summarize the evidence you have gathered to support your claim and explain your reasoning.

Checkpoints

Answer the following questions to check your understanding of the lesson.

3. Which of the following would be the best choice to model what drives surface ocean currents?

    A. a tank of water with a block of ice attached to one end

    B. a tank of water with a fan blowing over the surface of the water

    C. a system of pipes with a heater at one end

    D. a tank of water with a heater under the tank

4. Fill in each blank with *increases* or *decreases* to show how the density of liquid ocean water can change.

    A. Rain falls into the ocean; the density of ocean water _____.

    B. Ocean water cools from 30 °C to 25 °C; the density of ocean water _____.

    C. A river empties into the ocean; the density of ocean water _____.

Use the map to answer Questions 5–6.

5. The map shows the surface temperature of the Gulf Stream and the ocean water farther north. Where are deep currents most likely to be forming as water from the surface sinks?

    A. south of 30° north latitude

    B. between 30° and 35° north latitude

    C. between 35° and 40° north latitude

    D. north of 40° north latitude

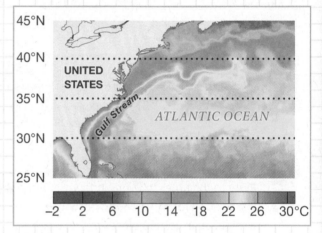

6. Thermal energy is transferred from the warm Gulf Stream ocean water to the cooler air above it by the process of *conduction / convection / radiation.*

Use the map to answer Questions 7–8.

7. Which statement explains why the water in the South Pacific gyre begins to warm up as it moves away from the coast of South America?

    A. It receives more energy from the sun.

    B. It receives more rainfall from the atmosphere.

    C. It loses more thermal energy to the atmosphere.

8. Ocean water in the *cold / warm* Peru Current is deflected by the continent of *South America / Antarctica / Australia* and then joins the South Equatorial Current.

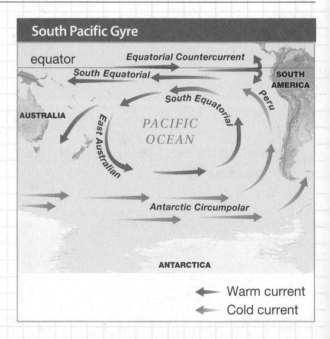

Interactive Review

Complete this section to review the main concepts of the lesson.

Surface currents are affected by wind, by the Coriolis effect, and by continental deflection.

A. Explain how energy that comes from outside the Earth system drives the flow of water in surface currents.

Deep ocean currents form when denser ocean water sinks. The flow of deep currents is also affected by the Coriolis effect and by continental deflection.

B. Draw a diagram that models one way a deep current could form.

Global ocean circulation moves water through Earth's ocean basins and plays an important role in the cycling of matter and the flow of energy in the Earth system.

C. Explain how the flow of matter and energy in global ocean circulation is related to interactions of the ocean with two other parts of the Earth system.

Interactions in Earth's Systems Cause Weather

Heavy rain falls from this dramatic storm cloud that formed where hot and cold air masses met.

Explore First

Measuring Wind Direction   Build a device that you can set up to measure wind direction outside your home or school. Be sure to place your device where objects such as buildings or trees will not influence your measurements. Does the wind blow in the same direction most of the time or does it change? How might you improve your device?

CAN YOU EXPLAIN IT?

What could cause a storm like this to happen suddenly?

It was a calm and cloudy spring day in this Utah town. Suddenly the clouds grew dark and heavy, and a storm covered the town in a blanket of snow.

Explore Online

1. What could cause the weather to change suddenly like this?

2. **Draw** Include a drawing to illustrate your explanation.

EVIDENCE NOTEBOOK As you explore this lesson, gather evidence to help explain what causes sudden changes in weather like this storm.

Describing Weather

Elements of Weather

Has weather ever caused your plans to change? **Weather** is a description of the short-term conditions of the atmosphere at a particular time and place. Reports of weather might include information about temperature, humidity, precipitation, air pressure, wind speed, and cloud cover.

3. What is the weather like right now? What is your favorite kind of weather? What is your least favorite kind of weather?

Temperature

Temperature is a measure of how hot or cold something is, which has to do with the motion of the particles that make up matter. So, the temperature of air is related to the kinetic energy of air particles. The faster the air particles move, the greater their kinetic energy is. Look at the models of cool and warm air particles within a cube. The air in each cube is under the same amount of pressure.

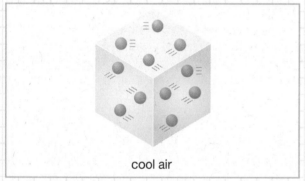

cool air

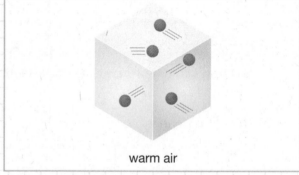

warm air

The cool air particles in this cube move more slowly and have less kinetic energy than the air particles in the warm air cube.

In the same volume of warm air, the particles move faster and are more spread out. Warm air is less dense than cool air.

Humidity

Humidity is a measure of the amount of water vapor in the air. Much of the water vapor in air comes from the evaporation of liquid water on Earth's surface. The more water vapor there is in the air, the higher the humidity of the air is. Humidity affects how warm or cool you feel. You might feel comfortable at 25 °C, but if the humidity rises, you may feel too warm, even if the temperature is the same.

Weather reports often refer to relative humidity. *Relative humidity* is the percentage of water vapor in air relative to the amount needed to saturate the air at the same temperature. For example, at 10 °C, air becomes saturated when there are 8 grams of water vapor per kilogram of air (g/kg). At this point, the relative humidity is 100%. If there were only 4 g/kg of water vapor in the air at 10 °C, then the relative humidity would be 50%. The warmer the air is, the more water vapor it can contain without reaching saturation.

Clouds and Precipitation

What happens when relative humidity exceeds 100%? At this point, more water vapor condenses than evaporates. The water vapor condenses onto particles in the air, such as dust and pollen, to form liquid water droplets or ice crystals. These droplets and crystals form clouds. The droplets and ice crystals in clouds grow and fall back to Earth as precipitation, such as rain, snow, hail, or sleet. The type of precipitation that forms and falls depends on the air temperature where the cloud formed and the changing air temperature as the precipitation falls to the ground.

Clouds themselves affect the air temperature. During the day, clouds can keep an area cool by reflecting more sunlight back into space. Clouds also affect temperatures overnight. During the day, energy from the sun is converted into thermal energy as it warms Earth. Earth radiates some of the thermal energy it absorbed during the day back toward space. If no clouds are present at night, much of this thermal energy escapes into space and cooler temperatures result. If clouds are present, they may absorb the thermal energy and radiate it back down to Earth's surface. This is why a cloudy night is often warmer than a clear night.

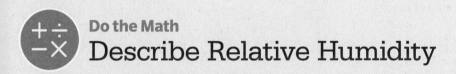

Do the Math
Describe Relative Humidity

The line on this graph shows how much water vapor is in the air at 100% relative humidity at different temperatures. For example, at 30 °C, relative humidity reaches 100% when there are 29 grams of water in each kilogram of air.

4. Use the graph to circle the word that correctly completes each sentence.

   A. As temperature increases, it takes more / less water vapor to reach 100% relative humidity.

   B. At 25 °C with 10 g/kg of water vapor in the air, precipitation is likely / not likely.

   C. If 10 g/kg of water vapor remained in the air and the temperature dropped to 10 °C, precipitation would be likely / not likely.

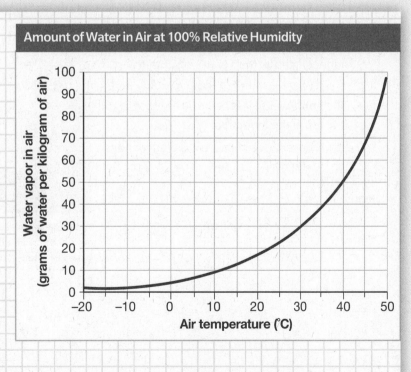

Amount of Water in Air at 100% Relative Humidity

5. Think about the storm that swept over the town in Utah. How did the clouds and snow form? Record your evidence.

Air Pressure

Particles of air are invisible, but they do have mass. Gravity pulls the particles toward Earth's surface. Air particles press on objects from all sides. *Air pressure* is the force of air pushing on an object.

The air pressure on any one object on Earth depends on how much air exists above that object. The more air there is above an object, the greater the air pressure will be. Air pressure is measured in millibars (mb). At sea level, the air pressure is about 1,013 mb. Higher above sea level, less air is above you, so the air pressure will be lower. For example, the air pressure on the top of Mount Everest is only 300 mb.

6. A student drank a bottle of water during a car ride up a mountain. At the top of the mountain, the student capped the plastic bottle. During the drive back down the mountain, what might happen to the bottle?

   A. It will expand because the air pressure is lower at the bottom of the mountain.

   B. It will contract because the air pressure is higher at the bottom of the mountain.

   C. It will become lighter. The air particles in the bottle weigh less because they are from the top of the mountain.

   D. It will not change because it is empty and contains no air.

At low elevations, air particles are packed together because the weight of the air above them is greater. At high elevations, there is less air above, so the particles are more spread out.

Wind

Air flows from high to low pressure. For example, air from an opened balloon will escape from the high air pressure inside the balloon to the lower air pressure outside the balloon. This movement of air is called *wind*. The greater the air pressure difference is between two places, the faster the air moves and the stronger the wind is.

7. Draw an arrow in the middle box to show which way the wind is blowing. Add the labels high pressure and low pressure on either side of the photo.

Air moves because of differences in air pressure.

Language SmArts
Describe Weather

8. Think back to the descriptions you wrote about the current weather, your favorite weather, and your least favorite weather. Choose one description and apply what you have learned to rewrite that description. Include the terms *temperature, humidity, precipitation, wind,* and *air pressure*.

_____
_____
_____
_____
_____

9. What might have caused the type of weather in your description? For example, why might it have been sunny, rainy, or windy?

_____
_____
_____
_____
_____
_____

Identifying Weather Associated with Pressure Systems

Air temperature varies because the sun warms Earth's surface unevenly. Because temperature affects pressure, differences in air temperature result in differences in air pressure. Differences in air pressure cause wind to blow. Wind moves clouds and precipitation from one place to another.

On weather maps, an "H" shows where the air pressure is highest. An "L" shows where it is lowest. An *isobar* is a line that connects points of equal air pressure. Observe the patterns in air pressure on the map.

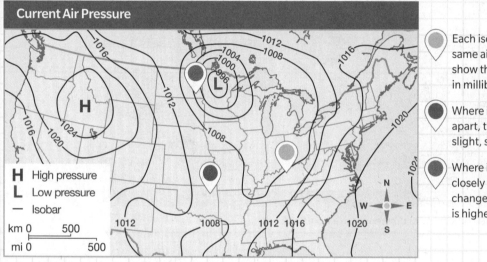

Current Air Pressure

H High pressure
L Low pressure
— Isobar
km 0   500
mi 0   500

Each isobar traces along the same air pressure. The numbers show the measured air pressure in millibars (mb).

Where isobars are spaced far apart, the air pressure change is slight, so wind speed is lower.

Where isobars are spaced closely together, the air pressure change is great, so wind speed is higher.

10. Draw a line across the map anywhere you choose. Describe how the air pressure and wind speed change as you go along this line.

11. Engineer It A team of engineers and meteorologists are working to identify the best places in the United States to build new wind farms. Because wind conditions can change from day to day, they conducted research to find the average wind speeds in the United States. What else might they need to consider to make a decision? Circle all that apply.

A. land ownership

B. average wind direction

C. frequency of storms

D. current wind speed

Pressure Systems

Examine the maps showing high- and low-pressure systems. A *high-pressure system* forms where air sinks toward the surface. As the air sinks, it spreads out from the high-pressure system toward areas of lower air pressure. Because Earth rotates, the air moves away from the high-pressure area in an outward spiral.

Where warm, less dense air rises from Earth's surface, a *low-pressure system* forms. This happens as air flows in from higher-pressure areas. The air moves into a low-pressure area as an inward spiral.

Pressure Systems and Weather

As air in a high-pressure systems sinks, it gets warmer. Relative humidity decreases, and if there were any clouds, they evaporate. These conditions usually bring clear skies and calm or gentle winds. In contrast, the air in a low-pressure system rises and cools. Clouds and rain form if the air is humid enough and the temperature drops enough.

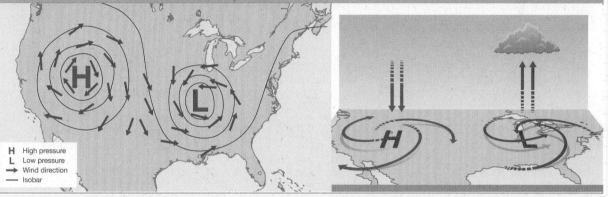

Air Pressure Systems in the Northern Hemisphere

Earth rotates, so wind does not blow in a straight line. In the Northern Hemisphere, air spirals counterclockwise around a low-pressure system and clockwise around a high-pressure system.

H High pressure
L Low pressure
→ Wind direction
— Isobar

12. Write H or L to indicate whether each statement is associated with a high-pressure system or a low-pressure system in the Northern Hemisphere.

H	sinking air becomes warmer
	rising air becomes cooler
	clear, sunny weather

	cloudy, rainy weather
	clockwise winds spread out
	counterclockwise winds move in

EVIDENCE NOTEBOOK

13. Think again about the storm that blew over the town in Utah. What kind of pressure system was probably involved? Record your evidence.

Interpret a Weather Map

A weather map shows the weather conditions of an area at a particular time. The map may include information, such as temperature, humidity, wind, cloud cover, precipitation, and air pressure.

14. This map shows precipitation and air pressure. Use the descriptions in the word bank to label the map and describe the weather associated with each pressure system.

> **WORD BANK**
> - sunny and calm
> - rainy
> - snowstorms, windy

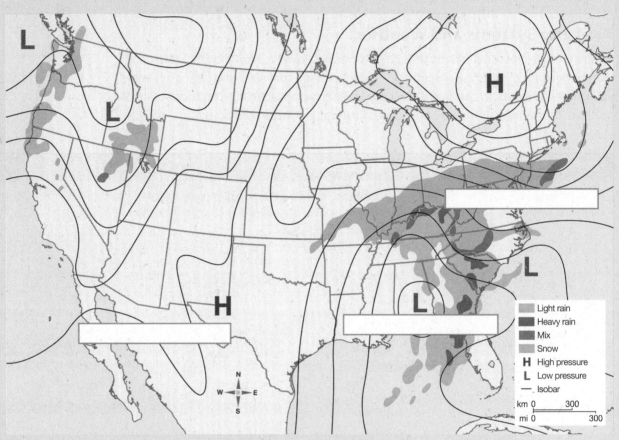

15. What patterns can you see in the map related to air-pressure systems and different weather conditions?

_____

_____

_____

_____

_____

_____

_____

_____

_____

_____

_____

Explaining How Fronts Change Weather

The Formation of Air Masses

An **air mass** is a large body of air that has similar temperature and humidity throughout it. An air mass develops over Earth's surface when air stays in one region for many days or weeks. The air mass gradually takes on the characteristics of the water or land below it. An air mass that forms above a warm, dry desert will be warm and dry. An air mass that forms above Arctic waters will be cool and humid.

WORD BANK
~~warm and dry~~
warm and humid
cool and dry
cool and humid

16. What kind of air mass do you think forms over each region shown in the photos? Use the descriptions in the word bank to label each photo.

warm and dry

The Movement of Air Masses

Eventually, air masses move because of air pressure differences. As an air mass travels, its temperature and humidity can slowly change as conditions on Earth's surface below the air mass change. When two different air masses meet, the warmer air mass will generally rise over the cooler air mass.

Along the California coast in summer, the water is cool. Therefore, cool and humid air masses form over the area. These air masses often move toward land and run into hot and dry air masses. Think about how summer weather patterns might depend on distance from the coast.

Hands-On Lab
Model an Air Mass Interaction

You will make a prediction about how a model will show the interaction between a warm and a cool air mass. You will then construct the model and use your observations to explain how warm and cool air masses interact.

MATERIALS

• container, shoebox-sized, clear, plastic
• food coloring, red
• ice cubes that contain blue food coloring
• water, warm

Procedure

STEP 1 The melted blue ice cubes represent a cold air mass, and the warm red water represents a warm air mass. Read through this procedure, and then use what you know about air masses to write a prediction about what might happen when the blue and red water interact.

STEP 2 Fill the plastic container half full of warm water. Let the water settle and become still.

STEP 3 On one side of the container, carefully place the blue ice cubes into the warm water.

STEP 4 On the other side of the container, add a few drops of red food coloring.

STEP 5 Observe the interaction between the blue and red water. Record your observations.

Analysis

STEP 6 Was your prediction supported by your observations? Explain.

STEP 7 What type of weather might occur if these were two air masses interacting? Explain your thinking.

STEP 8 **Discuss** Is this a good model for showing how two air masses interact? Explain why or why not.

The Formation of Fronts

When two air masses of different temperatures and densities meet but do not mix, a front forms. A **front** is a boundary between air masses. The type of front that forms depends on the temperature, humidity, and motion of each air mass. The main types of fronts are cold fronts, warm fronts, stationary fronts, and occluded fronts.

Fronts commonly form as air masses rotate around low-pressure areas. As fronts move over Earth's surface, they cause changes in temperature and precipitation. A front might also change wind speed and direction as it passes over an area. Therefore, fronts have a strong effect on the weather.

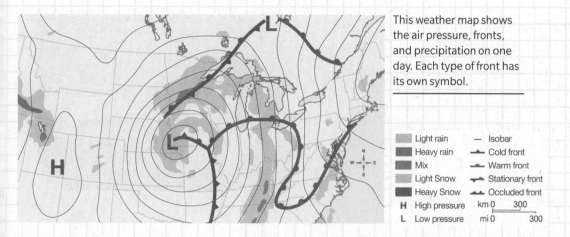

This weather map shows the air pressure, fronts, and precipitation on one day. Each type of front has its own symbol.

	Light rain		—	Isobar
	Heavy rain		▲	Cold front
	Mix		●	Warm front
	Light Snow		▼	Stationary front
	Heavy Snow		▲	Occluded front
H	High pressure		km 0 300	
L	Low pressure		mi 0 300	

Cold Fronts

A *cold front* is a boundary that forms as a cold air mass pushes under a warm air mass. A cold front is shown on a weather map by a blue line of triangles that point in the direction that the front is moving.

If the rising warm air is somewhat humid, scattered clouds form. If the rising warm air is very humid, heavy clouds and precipitation can occur. Cold fronts usually move quickly and can bring rain, snowstorms, and even thunderstorms. Cool, fair weather often follows a cold front.

Cold Front

cold air mass

warm air mass

Warm Fronts

A *warm front* forms where a warm air mass overrides a cold air mass. A warm front is shown on a map by a red line of half circles that point in the direction that the front is moving.

Warm fronts generally bring drizzly rain if the warm air mass is humid or scattered clouds if the air mass is only somewhat humid. Because warm air masses move slowly, the weather may remain rainy or cloudy for several days. After a warm front passes, the weather often becomes warmer.

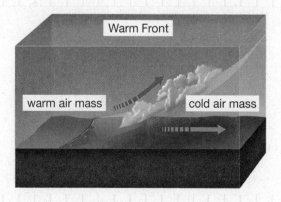

Warm Front

warm air mass

cold air mass

Stationary Fronts

A *stationary front* forms where a cold air mass and a warm air mass meet and become still. In other words, the air masses become stationary. A stationary front is represented on a map by alternating blue triangles and red half circles.

A stationary front often brings many days of clouds and precipitation. This happens as water vapor in the air along the boundary between the air masses rises and condenses.

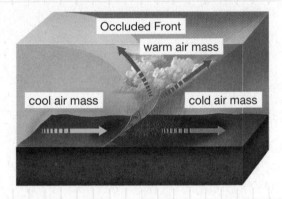

Occluded Fronts

An occluded front forms when a warm front gets pushed up under two cooler air masses. It is shown on a map as purple alternating triangles and half circles pointed in the direction the front is moving.

Because the warm air mass is pushed up, the temperature drops as an occluded front forms. Heavy precipitation can occur as water vapor in the warm air mass cools and condenses.

17. Fronts often form around areas of high / low pressure. A sudden thunderstorm is most likely associated with the arrival of a cold / warm / stationary front.

EVIDENCE NOTEBOOK

18. Which type of front is most likely associated with the weather change in the town in Utah? Record your evidence.

Language SmArts
Compare and Contrast Information

19. In the experiment, you modeled a cold front. Compare and contrast your model to the other media in the lesson that show cold fronts. Compare their strengths and weaknesses.

_____

_____

_____

_____

_____

_____

_____

Describing Weather Patterns in California

At a single moment in California, it can be hot and dry in one place and freezing and snowy in another place. The southern part of the state is closer to the equator and is generally warmer than the northern part. On the western side of the state lies the Pacific Ocean. On the eastern side of the state, the Sierra Nevada mountains influence temperature and precipitation patterns.

20. This satellite image shows densely vegetated areas in green. Drier, less vegetated areas are shown by brown and tan colors. Complete the paragraph to describe the satellite image.

    The satellite image shows
    dry / vegetated / hot areas along the Pacific coast and the *eastern / western* edge of the Sierra Nevada Mountains. These areas generally receive *more / less* precipitation than the brown areas *east / west* of California's Mountains, such as the Mojave Desert and the Great Basin.

21. With a partner, generate questions regarding the landforms and vegetation patterns you see in this satellite image. Think about how vegetation and precipitation are related.

Satellite Image of California and Nevada, July 2002

OREGON

CALIFORNIA   NEVADA

Great Basin

Sacramento Valley

Coast Range

Sierra Nevada Mtn

San Joaquin Valley

Mojave Desert

PACIFIC OCEAN

This satellite image of California shows areas where land is vegetated and where it is not.

Influences on Weather

Vegetation patterns can indicate the types of weather an area experiences. Weather is also influenced by vegetation. Trees can decrease wind speeds, release moisture into the air, and shade the ground. Several other interactions in the Earth system influence weather patterns as well. Driven by energy from the sun, these interactions between the biosphere, atmosphere, hydrosphere, and geosphere are constantly taking place. For example, California's weather patterns are influenced by interactions between the atmosphere and hydrosphere as solar energy causes ocean water to evaporate into the atmosphere. Upon cooling and condensing, the water vapor can form clouds, rain, fog, or snow that is brought to California by winds.

Prevailing Winds

Prevailing winds influence weather because they affect the speeds and directions of moving air masses. Prevailing winds tend to move west to east over the United States and Canada. These winds bring air masses from the Pacific Ocean toward California. Prevailing winds also drive ocean surface currents.

The Pacific Ocean

Along with gravity and differences in ocean water density, prevailing winds influence ocean currents that circulate around the globe. Just off the coast of California, a cold surface current called the California Current runs north to south.

Ocean surface currents affect weather in coastal cities. For example, the cold California Current carries cold water along California's coast. The air masses that form above this area are therefore cool and humid. Prevailing winds blow this air toward California. The cool, humid air interacts with landforms and inland air masses. The result is often fog, rain, and cool coastal temperatures in northern and central California.

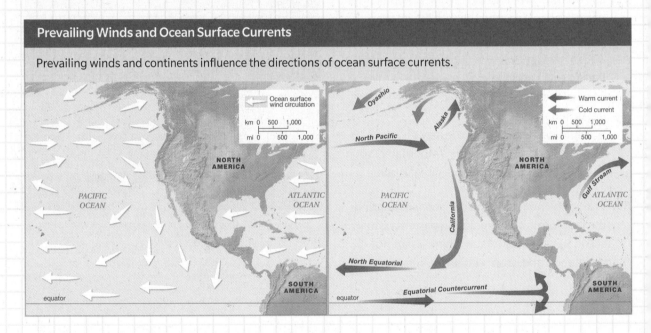

Prevailing Winds and Ocean Surface Currents

Prevailing winds and continents influence the directions of ocean surface currents.

22. Circle the correct terms to complete each statement.

Both prevailing winds and the continent of North America influence the direction of the North Pacific Current and the California Current. The California Current brings cold / warm ocean water along the coast of California.

Prevailing winds blow cool and humid air masses that form over the Pacific Ocean toward the east / west. Therefore, the Pacific Ocean is / is not a major influence on California's weather.

Landforms

Both prevailing winds and ocean surface currents are redirected as they run into land. For example, the California Current is partly a result of the North Pacific Current being deflected toward the south as it runs into North America.

A phenomenon known as the *rain shadow effect* happens where prevailing winds bring humid air over mountains. As the humid air is forced to rise over the mountains, it cools and condenses into clouds and causes precipitation. Once the air reaches the other side of the mountain, it is drier. Therefore, one side of the mountain is cloudy and has more precipitation. On the other side, it is dry and the skies are often sunny.

Pineapple Express Precipitation

The Pineapple Express is an *atmospheric river* that brings a huge amount of moisture from the tropical Pacific Ocean toward the western United States.

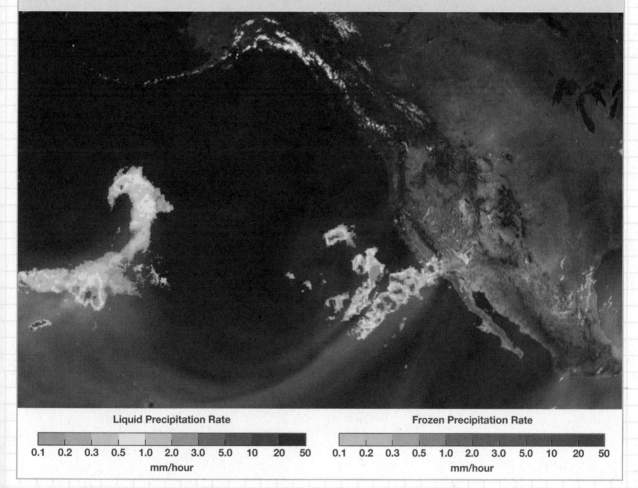

Liquid Precipitation Rate											Frozen Precipitation Rate										
0.1	0.2	0.3	0.5	1.0	2.0	3.0	5.0	10	20	50	0.1	0.2	0.3	0.5	1.0	2.0	3.0	5.0	10	20	50

mm/hour   mm/hour

23. Complete the following paragraph to explain how the Pineapple Express can cause extreme rainfall and snowfall in California.

In the tropical Pacific Ocean, warm ocean water enters the atmosphere by the process of *evaporation / condensation / precipitation.* Prevailing winds bring the moisture-filled air toward California, where it cools as it rises to pass over mountains. Water vapor in the cooling air *condenses / evaporates / disappears,* and precipitation falls. This is one example of how landforms, winds, and the ocean influence California's weather.

24. Think back to the satellite image of California and use the word bank to complete the description.

California's Coast Range forces humid air masses from the Pacific Ocean to rise and cool. This brings _____ weather and results in _____ vegetation on the western side of the Coast Range. On the eastern side, _____ air flows across the land and results in _____ vegetation.

Analyze Air Masses

Air masses form over large regions and move to new places due to air pressure differences. Air masses can change as they move. For example, a polar air mass moving over warm land will become warmer. Explore the map of air masses that influence weather in North America.

25. Weather changes as air masses meet and interact. Which air masses most likely influence weather in California? Use the map and your knowledge of air masses and prevailing winds to support your claim.

_____
_____
_____
_____
_____
_____
_____
_____
_____
_____
_____

Air Masses that Affect Weather in North America

Maritime Polar Pacific

Continental Polar Canadian

Maritime Polar Atlantic

PACIFIC OCEAN

UNITED STATES

ATLANTIC OCEAN

Maritime Tropical Pacific

Continental Tropic

Maritime Tropical Atlantic

Continue Your Exploration

Name: _____   Date: _____

Check out the path below or go online to choose one of the other paths shown.

Snowflake Sizes and Patterns	• El Niño and La Niña: Effects on Local Weather • Hands-On Labs 🖐 • Propose Your Own Path	*Go online to choose one of these other paths.*

Although snowflakes have a variety of structures, they all form by the same process. As air temperature cools, tiny droplets of water freeze and form ice crystals. Many crystals have a symmetrical pattern with six "arms." As the crystals fall toward Earth, water vapor in the atmosphere freezes onto the crystals and they grow larger.

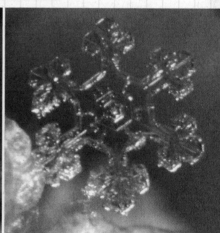

The unique shapes of individual snowflakes are a result of the temperatures in which they formed and fell to Earth. These ice crystals all have a similar 6-armed shape because they encountered similar conditions as the crystals fell through the atmosphere.

The Effects of Temperature and Humidity on Snowflakes

The variation in the shapes of snowflakes is a result of differences in air temperature and humidity. A crystal may begin to grow in one shape, but then as it falls through the atmosphere, changes in air temperature or humidity can cause it to grow in a different manner. For example, as air temperature increases during the snow crystal's descent, the sharper edges of a snowflake may become smoother.

The shape that the snow crystal has when it lands on a surface will determine the type of snow. Large snowflakes stack loosely on top of each other, leaving air pockets and producing fluffy, airy snow. Very cold temperatures and low humidity produce tiny snow crystals that can fall for hours and will barely build up. Warmer temperatures near freezing will produce heavy, wet snow.

Continue Your Exploration

The Effects of Temperature and Humidity on Snowflake Type

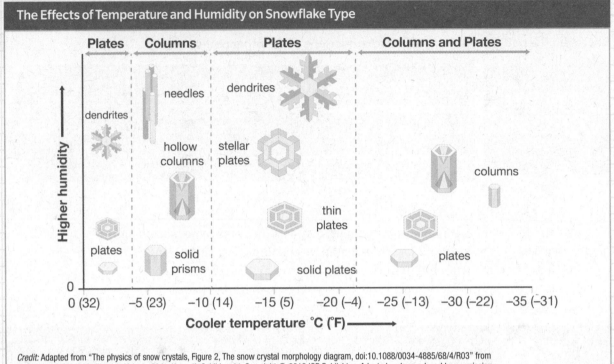

Credit: Adapted from "The physics of snow crystals, Figure 2, The snow crystal morphology diagram, doi:10.1088/0034-4885/68/4/R03" from Reports on Progress in Physics, Volume 68 by Kenneth G. Libbrecht. Copyright © 2012 IOP Publishing. Adapted and reproduced by permission of Kenneth G. Libbrecht and IOP Publishing Ltd.

1. What patterns do you notice in snowflake type and humidity across all temperatures?

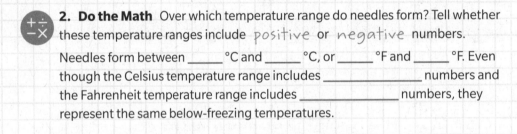

2. **Do the Math** Over which temperature range do needles form? Tell whether these temperature ranges include *positive* or *negative* numbers.

   Needles form between _____ °C and _____ °C, or _____ °F and _____ °F. Even though the Celsius temperature range includes _____ numbers and the Fahrenheit temperature range includes _____ numbers, they represent the same below-freezing temperatures.

3. What weather conditions might bring snow that is good for building a snow fort? Explain.

4. **Collaborate** Develop a list of interview questions and interview people about their experiences with winter weather. Take notes during each interview. Summarize your interviews into a short article, and be sure to use complete sentences.

Can You Explain It?

Name: _____   **Date:** _____

> ### What could cause a storm like this to happen suddenly?

EVIDENCE NOTEBOOK

Refer to the notes in your Evidence Notebook to help you construct an explanation for what causes sudden changes in weather like this storm.

1. State your claim. Make sure your claim fully explains how the storm suddenly occurred.

2. Summarize the evidence you have gathered to support your claim and explain your reasoning.

Checkpoints

Answer the following questions to check your understanding of the lesson.

Use the photo to answer Questions 3–4.

3. Differences in air humidity / pressure / pollution cause wind that blows snow across this landscape.

4. How did the cold front that caused this snowstorm form?

   A. Two warm air masses met.

   B. A cold air mass pushed up a warm air mass.

   C. Two cold air masses met.

   D. A warm air mass pushed up a cold air mass.

Use the map to answer Questions 5–6.

5. What type of weather do you notice near low-pressure areas?

   A. precipitation

   B. heat waves

   C. dry weather

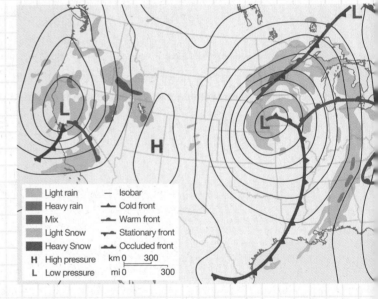

6. What does the distance between the isobars near the high-pressure area tell you?

   A. They are close together, so it is windy.

   B. They are far apart, so it is windy.

   C. They are far apart, so winds are calm.

   D. They are close together, so winds are calm.

7. Which factors would most likely affect the weather on a small, flat island in the ocean? Select all that apply.

   A. the formation of dry air masses

   B. ocean surface currents

   C. the formation of humid air masses

   D. the rain-shadow effect

8. Which is true about factors that influence weather?

   A. Precipitation type depends on air temperature.

   B. The rain shadow effect causes equal precipitation on both sides of a mountain.

   C. As air sinks, it absorbs moisture and forms rain clouds.

Interactive Review

Complete this section to review the main concepts of the lesson.

Temperature, humidity, and air pressure are factors that influence the weather we experience daily.

A. Explain how temperature and humidity are related and how that relationship impacts the weather.

High- and low-pressure systems affect wind speed and direction and are related to specific types of weather.

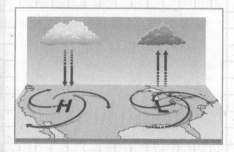

B. Why are low-pressure systems associated with rain but high-pressure systems are accompanied by clear skies?

Air masses take on characteristics of the regions over which they form. Moving air masses form fronts that affect the weather.

C. Provide an example of a front and explain how it forms.

California's weather is influenced by the Pacific Ocean, by landforms, and by prevailing winds.

D. How do mountains in California affect the weather?

Weather Predictions Are Based on Patterns

Weather prediction helps us prepare when we go outside.

Explore First

Analyzing Historical Weather Research what the weather was like on the day you were born. What was it like on your past birthdays? Describe any patterns you notice. Predict what the weather will be like next time your birthday comes around. What did you base your prediction on?

Go online to view the digital version of the Hands-On Lab for this lesson and to download additional lab resources.

CAN YOU EXPLAIN IT?

How does this forecaster know that stormy weather is coming?

This weather forecaster uses weather maps and charts to show her prediction that a cold front is going to bring heavy rain and storms to the area over the next five days.

Explore Online

1. How might this forecaster predict future weather conditions? Describe any data or tools she might use, and explain whether you think her prediction is likely to be accurate.

EVIDENCE NOTEBOOK As you explore this lesson, gather evidence to explain how weather predictions are made.

Using Mathematical Models to Make Predictions

Models in Science

How does an animal digest its food? Can a building withstand an earthquake? *Models* are tools that help scientists answer these kinds of difficult questions. Models are used in science to represent things that are large, small, dangerous, or complex. They help scientists make predictions and test ideas to find solutions to challenging questions.

It is possible for scientists to make models because events in nature often follow predictable patterns. For example, if you drop a ball from a certain height, you can predict how high it will bounce. Another pattern in nature is the yearly migration of some animals. Observing patterns in nature is the basis of science. These observations lead to explanations about the way the world works. Although these explanations are supported by observations, they may not be accurate. For example, the sun appears to move across the sky. For thousands of years, people observed this pattern and incorrectly concluded that Earth was the center of our solar system.

This model is called a *food web*. It uses arrows to show feeding relationships in an ecosystem. For example, rabbits eat grass and foxes eat rabbits.

2. Describe the food web by writing *increase* or *decrease*.

The rabbit population would _____ if the supply of grass became limited. This would happen because grass is a food source for rabbits. If the population of rabbits and mice decreased, the population of hawks would likely

_____.

3. Write one question that the nautilus model could be used to answer. Write one question that the satellite image could be used to answer.

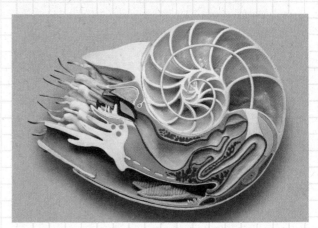

This model shows a cross-section of an animal called a nautilus. It has a shell made up of many chambers filled with gas to help the nautilus float. The nautilus fills its chambers with water when it wants to dive deeper.

This satellite image is a computer model that uses data about Earth. In the model, healthy vegetation stands out in red. Areas burned by wildfires are shown in black.

Mathematical Models

A *mathematical model* is a model that uses equations to represent the way a system or a process works. Some mathematical models are just a single equation. Others are more complex and involve many related equations. In order to use a mathematical model, data are collected. Next, data values are used to replace the variables of the equation or sets of equations in the model. Finally, calculations are made to get the results.

Mathematical Models and Prediction

Whether they are simple or complex, mathematical models can be used to make predictions. They can predict how something might work under different conditions. For example, you could use an equation to predict what an object would weigh on different planets. The equation is useful because we cannot easily travel to other planets and weigh the object. Mathematical models can also help to predict an event at a future time. Predictions can be shown on maps, graphs, and other displays.

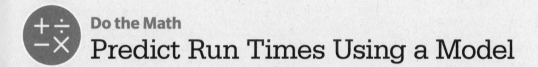

Do the Math
Predict Run Times Using a Model

Dwayne has been training for cross-country tryouts. He has been tracking his progress by recording his run times in a table every Saturday. In the left column, Dwayne noted the week number. In the right column, he noted his run times.

4. Plot the data from the table onto the graph.

Dwayne's Weekly One-Mile Run Times	
Time (week)	Run Time (min)
Week 1	11.95
Week 2	12.25
Week 3	11.40
Week 4	10.10
Week 5	9.25
Week 6	8.60

Dwayne's Weekly One-Mile Run Times

5. Dwayne's goal is to run 1 mile in 8 minutes or less. In order to predict when he will reach his goal, he drew a *trend line* that fits along the data points. He extended the trend line to week 8. According to the line, will he reach his goal by week 7? By week 8?

Trend in Dwayne's Weekly One-Mile Run Times

Did you know this line represents an equation? Another way to make a prediction about Dwayne's goal is to use the equation of the trend line:

$$y = -\frac{2}{3}x + 13$$

y = run time in minutes
x = time in weeks

The variable y represents Dwayne's run times. The variable x represents the week. To predict the run time for week 7, evaluate the equation for $x = 7$:

$$y = -\left(\frac{2}{3}\right)(7) + 13$$
$$y = 8.3 \text{ min}$$

The prediction is that Dwayne will be able to run a mile in 8.3 minutes by week 7. He will not have reached his goal.

6. Use the equation to predict if Dwayne will reach his goal by week 8. Compare your answer to the prediction that you made using the trend line on the graph.

Limitations of Mathematical Models

Models are important scientific tools, but they are limited because they are simplified versions of the systems they represent. All models, including the graph and equation used for Dwayne's running times, have limitations. If you solve the equation for week 15, the result is that he will run a mile in 3 minutes. It is not realistic that a person could run a mile in 3 minutes. Therefore, this model is only valid within a specific range of speeds.

Predict Costs Using a Model

You will use a mathematical model to make predictions.

    Suppose you are a manufacturer who must ship rope of four different lengths to a store. You would like to figure out your shipping costs. For this, you need to know the weight of each piece of rope. However, you do not have time to weigh each piece. You can measure a few samples of rope and use a mathematical model to predict the weight of materials and estimate your costs.

MATERIALS
- meterstick
- rope, pieces of different lengths (4)
- spring scale with 5 g increments

Procedure and Analysis

STEP 1 Select four pieces of rope of different lengths.

STEP 2 Measure the length in centimeters of all four pieces of rope. Record your measurements in the table.

STEP 3 Measure the weight in grams of three individual pieces of rope. Record your measurements in the table. Set those pieces of rope aside.

	Rope 1	Rope 2	Rope 3	Rope 4
Length (cm)				
Weight (g)	actual:	actual:	actual:	predicted: actual:

STEP 4 Make a graph that plots the length and weight of the three pieces of rope. Include a title and be sure to label your x-axis and y-axis.

STEP 5 Use your graph to predict the weight of the fourth piece of rope. Record your prediction in the table.

STEP 6 Explain how you used your graph to predict the weight of the fourth piece of rope.

STEP 7 You need to ship 10 pieces of each length of rope. Estimate the total weight of the ropes you will be shipping.

STEP 8 How much would the shipment cost if the shipping rate was $1.00 per 1000 grams? Round to the nearest cent.

STEP 9 Measure the actual weight of the fourth piece of rope. Record your measurement in the table.

STEP 10 Compare your prediction to the actual weight of the fourth piece of rope. Was your prediction accurate? Can you explain why or why not?

STEP 11 Would your estimate for the shipping cost change when using the actual weight of the fourth piece of rope? Explain why your prediction was still useful even if it was not completely accurate.

STEP 12 **Engineer It** If you were a manufacturer, you would want your method of prediction to be as accurate as possible. Can you think of a way to improve your method so that your predictions are more likely to be accurate?

Estimate Air Temperature with Cricket Chirps

Can crickets and a mathematical model help us estimate the temperature? Since the late 1800s, different equations have been developed to calculate the temperature based on the number of chirps a cricket makes over time. It was found that only certain species of crickets make reliable thermometers. The following equation works between 55–100 °F.

Snowy tree cricket chirp equation:
$T = N + 40$

Variables:

T = temperature (°F)

N = number of chirps every 13 seconds

This snowy tree cricket chirps at a different rate depending on the temperature outside! However, other things affect these crickets' chirp rates, such as age and mating behavior.

 7. A student recorded 39 chirps in 13 seconds around 4 p.m. Use the equation to estimate the temperature.

8. The actual temperature was measured at 4 p.m., and it was 76.6 °F. Explain why your estimate may have been different. Note any other limitations this model might have.

9. The hourly temperature forecast for the evening is 70 °F at 5 p.m., 64 °F at 6 p.m., and 62 °F at 7 p.m. Predict the rate at which the crickets will chirp at these times as the sun sets. Start by rearranging the equation to solve for N: $N = T - 40$.

Explaining the Accuracy of Weather Prediction

Weather Prediction

Have you ever seen a weather forecast online or in a newspaper? A **weather forecast** is a prediction about the state of the atmosphere at a given place and time. Weather forecasts are commonly provided using maps and weather charts. They can include predictions about temperature, wind, precipitation, cloud cover, and humidity. Have you ever used a weather forecast to make plans or decide what to wear? Weather forecasts not only help people plan their day, but they also provide warnings about severe weather, such as blizzards and hurricanes. Pilots also rely on forecasts to navigate the planes we fly in. Who else might use weather forecasts?

10. This weather chart shows past and current temperatures. Try to predict the temperature for Friday.

Monday	Tuesday	Wednesday	Thursday (today)	Friday (tomorrow)
5 °F	0 °F	1 °F	−2 °F	

11. What did you base your prediction on? What other data would you want to use if you were asked to predict the weather?

12. Do you think your prediction would be within a degree of the actual temperature? Within three degrees? Within five degrees? Explain your answer.

Data Used in Weather Prediction

To make a weather forecast, past and current weather conditions are considered. This includes things such as wind speed, air pressure, humidity, cloud cover, precipitation, and temperature. Also taken into account are the current locations and movements of air masses, fronts, and high- and low-pressure systems.

Weather Forecast for Truckee, California			
Wednesday Nov. 25	**Thursday** Nov. 26	**Friday** Nov. 27	This row shows predictions for the high and low temperatures along with a description of the predicted weather for each day.
HIGH **50 °F** LOW 35 °F Partly Sunny	**34 °F** 30 °F Cloudy, Chance of Rain	**26 °F** 18 °F Snowstorm	
Chance of Precipitation 0%	Chance of Precipitation 30%	Chance of Precipitation 90%	**Precipitation** This is the predicted chance of precipitation.
Wind ↗ southwest 14 mi/h	Wind ↑ south 16 mi/h	Wind ↙ northeast 20 mi/h	**Wind** Predicted wind speed is shown in miles per hour. Wind direction is shown with an arrow.
Humidity 26%	Humidity 68%	Humidity 94%	**Humidity** This is the predicted relative humidity.

Weather Forecast Models

Past and current weather data are used to build weather forecast models. Weather forecast models are based on the physical laws that determine how the atmosphere works. They are mathematical models that contain many related equations. The equations represent the atmosphere and its interactions in the Earth system. Because so many factors influence weather, forecast models are very complex. For example, ocean currents affect humidity in some locations, and humidity impacts precipitation and cloud cover.

In the early 1900s, the first weather forecast model was used. It took so long to do the calculations by hand that, by the time the forecast was ready, the weather had already happened. By the 1950s, computers could do these calculations more quickly. Today, supercomputers do them even faster. Five-day forecasts can be made with about the same level of certainty as a two-day forecast could thirty years ago. This is due to the continual improvement of weather forecast models and the increased speed of supercomputers. Meteorologists and forecasters analyze weather forecast model results before the results are shared with the public.

EVIDENCE NOTEBOOK

13. How do forecasters use mathematical models to make predictions about future weather conditions? Record your evidence.

Limitations of Weather Forecast Models

All weather predictions contain some degree of uncertainty—that is, they rarely turn out to be 100% accurate. Weather is a complex phenomenon that is affected by many factors. One small change in a factor, such as wind direction, can affect many other factors and result in different weather conditions. Because it is hard to predict the exact timing or location of future weather events, weather forecasts involve probabilities and percentages. For example, you may see a forecast that describes the probability of rain occurring for a specific area and time. This probability is often given as a percentage.

Weather forecast models are constantly being improved. Predictions are compared to what actually happens with the weather. For example, if a forecast predicted the temperature on Friday, the observed temperature on Friday is compared to the prediction. This comparison process would be followed for many days. If the predictions mostly match the recorded temperatures, then the model is a good predictor of temperature. If the model often predicts that it will be warmer or cooler than it actually is, then adjustments are made to improve the model. This process repeats as models are constantly improved to make predictions more likely to be accurate. Models are also improved in order to make predictions further into the future.

14. Look back to the forecast chart and maps for Truckee. Compare these predictions to what actually happened with the weather. Describe your findings. If the forecast chart did not predict exactly what happened with the weather, explain why it is still useful.

Weather Observations in Truckee, California

This weather chart shows past weather in Truckee. These weather data were recorded for the same days the predictions were made.

Wednesday Nov. 25	Thursday Nov. 26	Friday Nov. 27
HIGH **49 °F**	**32 °F**	**29 °F**
LOW 35 °F	29 °F	22 °F
Mostly Sunny	Fog, Rain, and Snow Mix	Rain and Snow Mix
Precipitation Amount 0.00 in.	Precipitation Amount 0.52 in.	Precipitation Amount 1.21 in.
Wind ↗ southwest 15 mi/h	Wind ↑ south 17 mi/h	Wind ↙ northeast 21 mi/h
Humidity 48%	Humidity 90%	Humidity 90%

EVIDENCE NOTEBOOK

15. Why do weather forecast models have limitations? Why are they still useful to people? Record your evidence.

16. Interpret the weather forecast maps to complete the descriptions.

These maps show the past / predicted / current weather. There is a cold / warm / stationary front moving toward Texas. This front is a boundary where a cold air mass is moving beneath a warm air mass and causing the warm air to rise. From Thursday to Friday, you can see that precipitation along this front increases / decreases / stays the same.

Two-Day Weather Forecast Model Results

These weather forecast maps were produced on a Wednesday. The maps show data resulting from a computer model that predicts the movement of fronts, pressure systems, and precipitation. The model also predicts how heavy the precipitation will be.

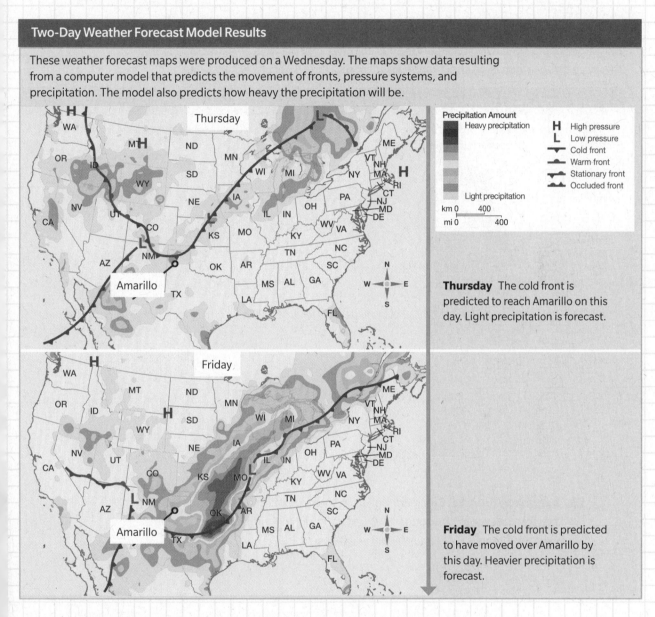

Thursday The cold front is predicted to reach Amarillo on this day. Light precipitation is forecast.

Friday The cold front is predicted to have moved over Amarillo by this day. Heavier precipitation is forecast.

17. Act Analyze the maps with a partner and act as meteorologists who are planning to deliver a weather forecast for Amarillo, Texas on Wednesday night. Explain how Amarillo's weather will change on Thursday and Friday.

18. Complete the descriptions to explain the limitations of the weather forecast model that produced these maps.

The accuracy of the model's results decrease with time into the future. Therefore, the forecast results for Thursday are likely to be more / less accurate than they will be for Friday. The model shows the type / amount / rate of precipitation with different colors, but the model does not give an exact quantity.

Analyze Weather Forecasts

Different models are used to predict weather for different ranges of time.

- Short-range weather forecasts make predictions for 0 to 3 days into the future.
- Medium-range weather forecasts make predictions for 3 to 7 days into the future.
- Long-range weather forecasts, or *outlooks*, range from weeks to months into the future.

In general, short-range forecasts are more likely to be accurate than forecasts made for longer periods of time. Given the continuous changes that occur in all of the factors that influence the weather, even short-range forecast results are not always accurate.

24-Hour Probability of Precipitation

This map shows how likely precipitation is over the next 24 hours. Notice that the map does not specify the amount or the type of precipitation.

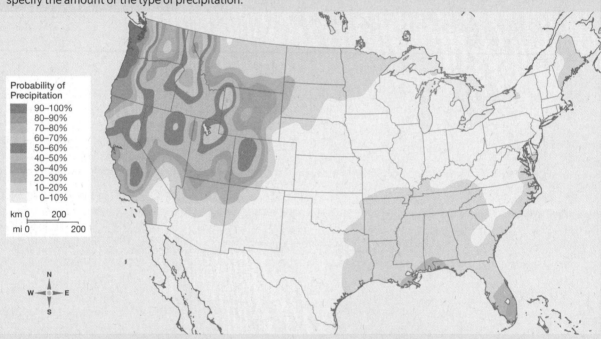

19. **Language SmArts** Cite evidence from the text and this map to explain how this forecast could be useful. How confident do you think the meteorologist using this map is that this forecast will be accurate?

_____

_____

_____

_____

_____

20. Based on this map, what travel advice would you give to someone planning to visit the beach in Oregon tomorrow?

_____

_____

_____

_____

Continue Your Exploration

Name: _____   Date: _____

Check out the path below or go online to choose one of the other paths shown.

People in Science

- **Hurricane Prediction**
- **Hands-On Labs**
- **Propose Your Own Path**

Go online to choose one of these other paths.

J. Marshall Shepherd, Meteorologist and Climatologist

Dr. J. Marshall Shepherd, who works at the University of Georgia, has been interested in weather since he made his own weather instruments for a school science project. Although the instruments he uses today, such as computers and satellites, are much larger and much more powerful than the instruments he made in school, they give him some of the same information.

In his work, Dr. Shepherd tries to understand weather events and relate them to current weather and climate change.

Do Cities Affect Rainfall?

Rainfall patterns are influenced by many factors, such as latitude, prevailing winds, and ocean currents. Some places are rainy because they are near an ocean or because they are located at certain latitudes. Other places are dry. For example, many deserts exist at 30 degrees latitude, both north and south of the equator. Dr. Shepherd and other scientists noticed increased rainfall in cities and in areas downwind of cities. For example, there was a 10-year thunderstorm study done in Atlanta, Georgia. The results, given in 2010, showed that during the summer months, there was an increase in rainfall and lightning over the city and downwind of the city, but not over the surrounding areas.

Continue Your Exploration

One explanation for the increased rainfall in cities is that dark surfaces, such as asphalt, absorb more energy from the sun than surfaces in a natural landscape do. Average temperatures in cities can be 6–8°F (3–4°C) warmer than the temperatures in natural landscapes surrounding a city. The warmer city surfaces warm the air directly above them. Because cities affect air temperature, they affect rainfall patterns. As warm air rises into the atmosphere, it begins to cool down. Moisture in the air forms clouds and brings rain to the city and to places downwind of the city, as seen in the Atlanta, Georgia, study. Another explanation is that cities disrupt air flow because of the tall buildings. Just like air rises over a tall mountain and causes rainfall, city buildings may have a similar effect.

1. One of the cities Dr. Shepherd has studied is Houston, Texas. He found that it rains more in Houston than in surrounding areas. What do you think will happen to rainfall amounts if Houston grows larger?

   A. Rainfall amounts will likely decrease in the city.

   B. Rainfall amounts will likely increase in the city.

   C. Rainfall amounts will likely be the same in the city.

2. **Draw** Make a diagram to show how cities might affect rainfall patterns. Include how a city's landscape impacts the flow of energy and the cycling of water.

3. A physical model is a miniature version of some part of the real world. How could you model how a city affects weather? Describe your physical model. What might you use to represent the sun, wind, rain, city surfaces, and natural surfaces?

4. **Collaborate** Research the historical weather data for a city that has grown very quickly over the past century. Are there any patterns in the precipitation data over time? Do you notice any other weather patterns that change over time? Record your observations. Share your results with a partner.

Can You Explain It?

Name: _____   **Date:** _____

How does this forecaster know that stormy weather is coming?

EVIDENCE NOTEBOOK

Refer to the notes in your Evidence Notebook to help you construct an explanation about how weather predictions are made.

1. State your claim. Make sure your claim fully explains how this forecaster predicted the weather, including any data or tools she might have used. Describe how accurate you think her forecast will be.

2. Summarize the evidence you have gathered to support your claim and explain your reasoning.

Checkpoints

Answer the following questions to check your understanding of the lesson.

Use the graph to answer Questions 3–4.

3. Using a ruler, draw a single, straight trend line that comes as close as possible to all the points, and extend it to day 40. How tall will the seedling be on day 40 according to your trend line model?

   A. 42 cm

   B. 32 cm

   C. 38 cm

   D. 34 cm

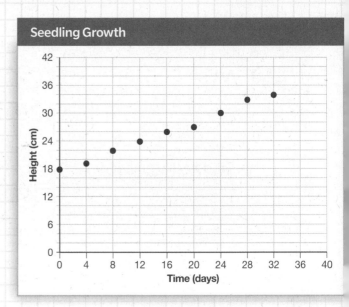

Seedling Growth

4. All models have limitations / graphs. By drawing a straight trend line on this graph, we are assuming the rate of growth is constant / changing. If the rate of growth changes as the plant ages, the line would / would not be straight and this model would not make a reliable prediction.

Use the map to answer Questions 5–6.

5. Currently, it is snowing in Fargo / Knoxville. It is likely to rain in Denver / Knoxville tomorrow because a cold / warm front is moving toward that area.

6. Rate the following forecast statements from 1 to 3, with 1 being the most likely to be accurate and 3 being the least likely to be accurate.

   _____ Tomorrow, it will be snowy in Fargo.

   _____ In seven days, it will be sunny in Denver.

   _____ In four days, it will be rainy in Knoxville.

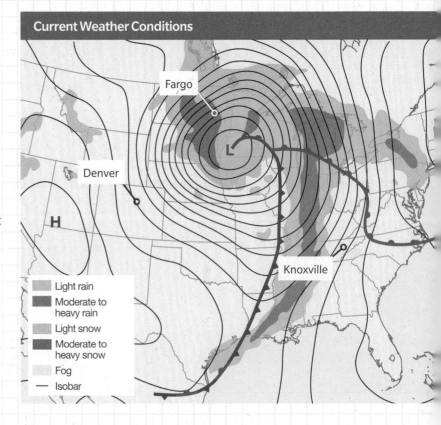

Current Weather Conditions

Fargo

L

Denver

H

Knoxville

Light rain
Moderate to heavy rain
Light snow
Moderate to heavy snow
Fog
— Isobar

Interactive Review

Complete this section to review the main concepts of the lesson.

Mathematical models include equations that represent processes or phenomena. All mathematical models have limitations.

A. Why are mathematical models so valuable to scientists who study complex phenomena like weather?

Weather forecasts are made by analyzing various weather data and determining the probability that certain weather conditions will exist in the future based on patterns.

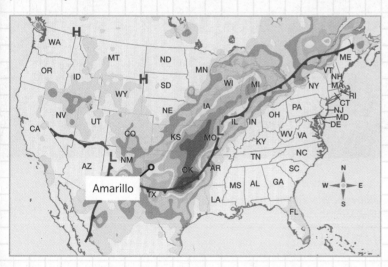

B. Weather forecast models have advantages and drawbacks. For example, one model may predict rain in a region with more accuracy than another model. Explain how the accuracy of a weather forecast model is tested.

Earth Has Different Regional Climates

These alpine wildflowers thrive in the cool and dry air in the Sierra Nevada Mountains.

Explore First

Observing Organisms Make a list of plants and animals you see in your local area. Compare your list with your classmates' lists. Discuss what factors might determine the types of plants and animals that live in your area. How are they affected by weather conditions? Do the plants and animals you see change with the seasons?

Go online to view the digital version of the Hands-On Lab for this lesson and to download additional lab resources.

CAN YOU EXPLAIN IT?

Why do these regions in California have such different climates?

Yosemite National Park is part of the Sierra Nevada Mountains. The park has cold, snowy winters and dry, short summers with temperatures that rarely reach 90 °F. There are pine forests, bears, deer, rivers of fish, and many kinds of birds. Two glaciers currently exist at the highest elevations.

Joshua Tree National Park is in the Mojave Desert. It is dry year-round. The park has very hot summers, and winters are mild with daytime temperatures in the 60s and 70s. Desert plants, such as this yucca, also known as a Joshua tree, are found here. The park is also home to many reptiles and birds as well as nocturnal animals such as coyotes, snakes, and rabbits.

1. Why do you think short-term and long-term weather conditions are different in different locations around the world?

2. Explore the photos and captions to identify differences between these parks. List your observations.

EVIDENCE NOTEBOOK As you explore the lesson, gather evidence to help explain why the climates in these two locations are so different.

Describing Climate

The world has many different climates. The average weather in an area over a long period is called **climate**. Descriptions of climate usually include temperature, precipitation averages, and sometimes information about winds, clouds, and seasons.

This area near Lake City, Colorado, is popular for ice climbers. The area has long, cold winters that are partially due to its high elevation.

The Tottori sand dunes in Japan exist because prevailing winds have continuously blown sand inland from Japan's coastline.

Surfers enjoy the Pacific Ocean and the mild, sunny climate in San Clemente, California. On average, there are 281 sunny days per year in this area.

3. **Discuss** Are there popular sports or outdoor activities where you live due to the climate?

Climate of San Francisco, California

This graph shows San Francisco's average monthly temperatures and precipitation totals. These averages were calculated over a long period of time, from 1981 to 2010.

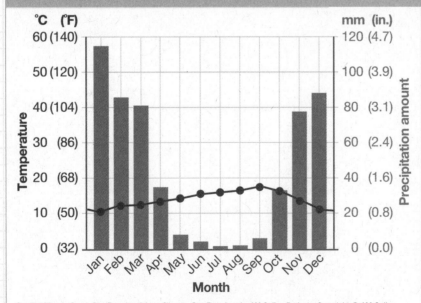

Temperature The red line on the graph shows that the average temperature does not vary much over the year. It stays between 10 °C and 20 °C.

Precipitation Unlike the average temperature, the average precipitation amount varies greatly over the year. The blue bars show that the precipitation amount is highest from November to March.

Credit: "Climate Graph San Francisco" from Climate: San Francisco by AM Online Projects. Copyright © AM Online Projects. Adapted and reproduced by permission of Alexander Merkel, AM Online Projects, © Climate-Data.org

4. This graph shows San Francisco's climate over a period of 1 / 10 / 30 years. The warmest month is January / July / September. The rainiest month is January / July / September.

Climate Descriptions

Climate descriptions include the average temperatures and precipitation amounts over many years. Precipitation is usually expressed as average monthly totals. Average monthly temperature is also included in climate descriptions, and sometimes includes the average high and low temperatures for each month. Climate may also be described by how windy, cloudy, or humid a place is. Finally, an area's climate description can include its seasons—or its lack of seasons.

Climate graphs are used to display average monthly rainfall and temperature data. By comparing climate graphs from two different places, we can describe similarities and differences about their climates. Climate graphs also allow us to make predictions. For example, a climate graph could help a person predict the best time of year to plan an outdoor event.

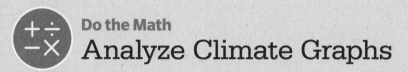

Do the Math
Analyze Climate Graphs

Imagine this: You won a trip to see the Great Wall of China, near the city of Beijing. To make sure that you can comfortably explore outside, you want to visit when the temperature is at or above 20 °C and when the chances of precipitation are low.

5. On the graph, circle the names of months with temperatures at or above 20 °C.

6. Of the months you circled, which month has the least amount of precipitation?

_____

7. The graph does not specify whether the precipitation is snow or rain. Use the graph to infer which time of year snow would fall and which time of year rain would fall. Explain your reasoning.

_____

_____

_____

_____

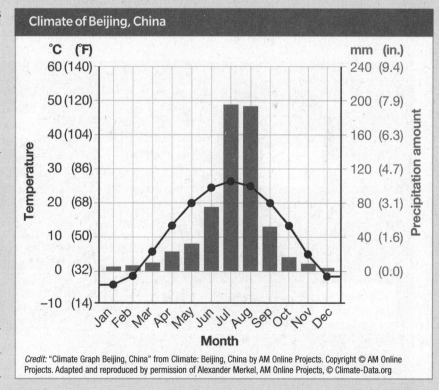

Credit: "Climate Graph Beijing, China" from Climate: Beijing, China by AM Online Projects. Copyright © AM Online Projects. Adapted and reproduced by permission of Alexander Merkel, AM Online Projects, © Climate-Data.org

Describing How Sunlight Affects Climate

Energy from the sun powers the Earth system and Earth's climate. The sun radiates energy. This energy travels in the form of waves and has to go about 150 million kilometers (93 million miles) through space before it reaches Earth. Energy enters the Earth system during the day when the sun is shining. Some of the energy is reflected and some is absorbed by Earth's surface and atmosphere.

8. Think about how the ground might feel on your bare feet on a sunny day. Do you think different surfaces, such as the grass, a sidewalk, or sand, would have the same temperatures? Why or why not?

Earth's Energy Balance

Earth emits the energy it absorbs as radiation. This emitted energy drives currents in Earth's oceans and atmosphere and powers the climate system. Eventually, most of the energy emitted by Earth leaves the Earth system and goes back into space. So, the amount of energy coming into the Earth system roughly equals the amount going out.

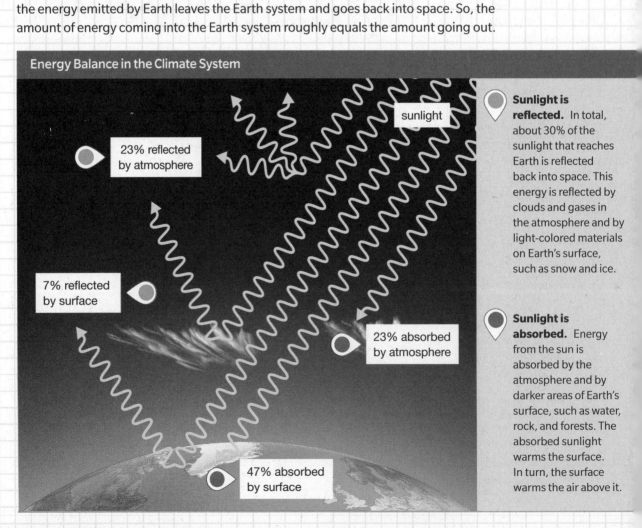

Energy Balance in the Climate System

sunlight

23% reflected by atmosphere

7% reflected by surface

23% absorbed by atmosphere

47% absorbed by surface

Sunlight is reflected. In total, about 30% of the sunlight that reaches Earth is reflected back into space. This energy is reflected by clouds and gases in the atmosphere and by light-colored materials on Earth's surface, such as snow and ice.

Sunlight is absorbed. Energy from the sun is absorbed by the atmosphere and by darker areas of Earth's surface, such as water, rock, and forests. The absorbed sunlight warms the surface. In turn, the surface warms the air above it.

Sunlight and Latitude

Latitude is the distance north or south of the equator. An area's climate depends on its latitude because latitude determines the intensity and amount of sunlight an area receives. Generally, areas that receive more direct sunlight are warmer than areas that receive less direct sunlight. Solar radiation arrives from the sun in essentially a straight line. However, because Earth's surface is curved, some of the sun's rays strike the surface more directly, while others strike at an angle.

9. **Collaborate** With a partner, model how sunlight strikes Earth. One person should shine a flashlight straight down onto a sheet of paper, and the other should trace the lighted area. Note the distance from the flashlight to the paper using a ruler. Next, shine the flashlight on a different area of the paper at the same distance away, but tilt the flashlight at an angle. Trace this shape. Explain how this models the way sunlight strikes Earth. Can you think of a way to improve this model? Explain.

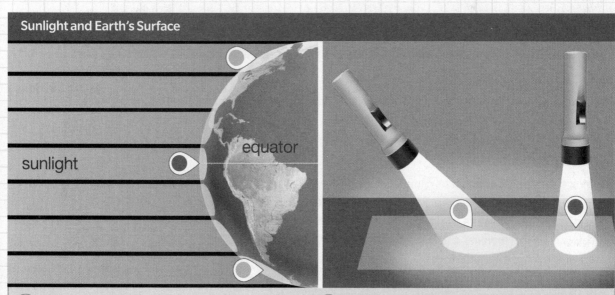

Sunlight and Earth's Surface

sunlight

equator

Near the equator, sunlight hits Earth most directly. Therefore, a certain amount of solar energy strikes a relatively small area. So, areas near the equator have higher temperatures than areas farther from the equator do. When the flashlight is shined perpendicularly to the paper, the light strikes a relatively small area.

Near the poles, sunlight hits Earth indirectly. The same amount of sunlight is therefore spread over a larger area than at the equator. As a result, areas near the poles have lower temperatures than areas near the equator do. When the flashlight is shined at an angle, the light is spread over a larger area.

Albedos of Earth's Surface

Different materials absorb and reflect different amounts of sunlight. *Albedo* describes how much sunlight a surface reflects. Generally, dark-colored surfaces absorb a lot of sunlight. That means dark surfaces do not reflect much sunlight and have low albedos. The absorbed energy warms the surfaces and the surfaces warm the air above them.

Light-colored surfaces generally reflect a lot of sunlight, so they have high albedos. Surfaces with high albedos stay relatively cool because they reflect so much sunlight. Because these surfaces are cool, the air above them stays cool, too.

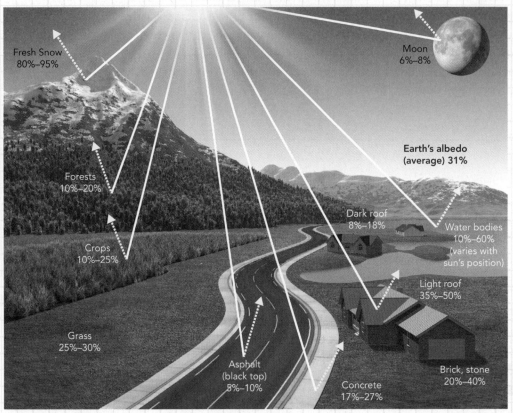

Fresh Snow
80%–95%

Forests
10%–20%

Crops
10%–25%

Grass
25%–30%

Asphalt
(black top)
5%–10%

Concrete
17%–27%

Moon
6%–8%

Earth's albedo
(average) 31%

Dark roof
8%–18%

Water bodies
10%–60%
(varies with
sun's position)

Light roof
35%–50%

Brick, stone
20%–40%

Light surfaces reflect more sunlight than dark surfaces do.

Credit: Adapted from Elemental Geosystems by Robert W. Christopherson. Copyright © 2007 by Pearson Education, Inc. Adapted and reproduced by permission of Pearson Education, Inc.

10. When humans build a parking lot of dark asphalt over a grassy field, the albedo of the surface _____. When ice and snow melt due to changes in climate, soil and rock are revealed and the albedo _____.

WORD BANK
- increases
- decreases

Albedo and Climate

A region's surface types affect its climate. In general, the more sunlight that is absorbed, the warmer the area will become. For example, in a city with a lot of dark surfaces, such as asphalt, the temperature can be a few degrees higher than the temperature in a nearby grassland. However, this is not always true. Think about a forest with a sandy desert nearby. You might think the forest would be warmer because the trees are darker than the sand. However, the forest could be cooler because its trees shade the ground and because trees use energy to release water from their leaves, which cools the air. The desert does not have any of these processes to lower temperatures.

EVIDENCE NOTEBOOK

11. How might the surface types in Yosemite and Joshua Tree National Parks affect their climates? Record your evidence.

Analyze Rooftop Albedos in Los Angeles

In cities, there are several human-made surfaces. Roofs, sidewalks, roads, and parking lots are often made up of materials such as asphalt and concrete. In a large city, such as Los Angeles, the colors of rooftops can have an impact on the local climate. Explore the map below to see the albedos of some of Los Angeles' rooftops.

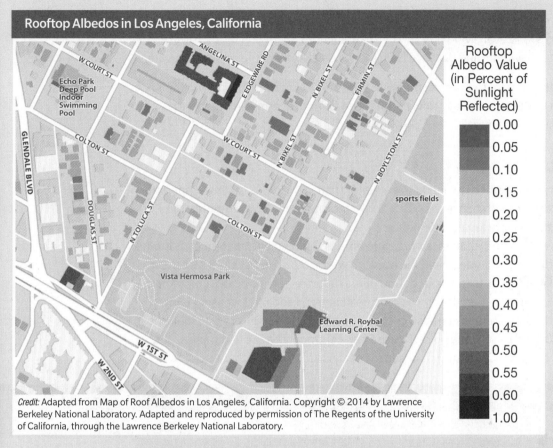

Rooftop Albedos in Los Angeles, California

Rooftop Albedo Value (in Percent of Sunlight Reflected)

0.00
0.05
0.10
0.15
0.20
0.25
0.30
0.35
0.40
0.45
0.50
0.55
0.60
1.00

Credit: Adapted from Map of Roof Albedos in Los Angeles, California. Copyright © 2014 by Lawrence Berkeley National Laboratory. Adapted and reproduced by permission of The Regents of the University of California, through the Lawrence Berkeley National Laboratory.

12. The red, orange, and yellow roofs on the map reflect 0–25% of sunlight. These roofs are likely *warmer / cooler* than the green and blue roofs.

13. Which of the following is likely true about the air temperatures near the red, orange, and yellow roofs compared to the air temperatures near blue and green roofs?

   A. The air temperatures are the same near all roofs.

   B. The air is slightly warmer near the red, orange, and yellow roofs.

   C. The air is slightly cooler near the red, orange, and yellow roofs.

14. **Engineer It** You are a part of a planning group that wants to make the air temperatures in this part of Los Angeles cooler. Use the data on this map and the information from the text to write a recommendation to help the group achieve this goal.

_____

_____

_____

_____

_____

_____

Explaining What Influences Climate

Factors That Influence Climate

A location's climate is influenced by interactions between the ocean, the atmosphere, ice, landforms, and even living things. These interactions are driven by energy from the sun. Latitude, elevation, and distance from the ocean also affect the climate of an area.

15. **Discuss** Compare today's weather with your area's climate. What do you think caused the weather today? How might those factors be similar to factors that determine the climate?

Latitude

The intensity of sunlight is greater at the equator than at the poles, so the temperature is higher at the equator than at the poles. Look at the diagram. These temperature differences cause air pressure differences.

Along with Earth's rotation, air pressure differences result in different global wind patterns at different latitudes. Near the equator, warm, moist air rises and cools, and water vapor condenses to form clouds and rain. Therefore, rainy climates commonly exist near the equator. A similar process occurs near 60°N and 60°S, causing rainy climates in those regions. In contrast, cool, dry air sinks along high-pressure belts near 30°N and 30°S and also at the poles. These areas commonly have dry climates. One reason why southern California has deserts is because the latitude there is 32°N.

Latitude's Effect on Climate Patterns

The intensity of sunlight at different latitudes results in different climates.

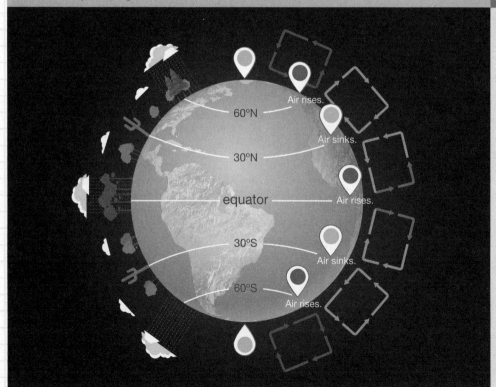

Explore Online

Around low-pressure belts, air rises, cools, and forms clouds and precipitation. Low-pressure belts result in wet climates.

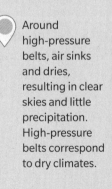
Around high-pressure belts, air sinks and dries, resulting in clear skies and little precipitation. High-pressure belts correspond to dry climates.

Prevailing Winds

Prevailing winds are global patterns of wind that generally move in a certain direction. Prevailing winds affect climate because they move air masses from one place to another. For example, moist air masses that form over the Pacific Ocean are carried to the west coast of the United States by prevailing winds called the *westerlies.* Prevailing winds also drive ocean surface currents that travel the globe and constantly move both warm and cool ocean water.

Distance from the Ocean

Water absorbs and releases energy more slowly than land does. As a result, oceans keep the temperature of nearby land from changing as much as it would if there were no water nearby. Because it is near the Pacific Ocean, California has a milder climate than states further inland, such as Nevada and Arizona.

Nearby bodies of water increase the humidity of nearby air. Because of this, places near large bodies of water often have more clouds and precipitation than they would if the body of water were not present.

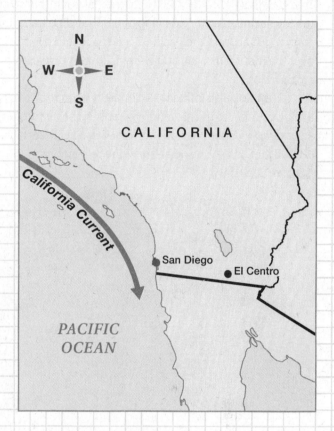

16. The average annual high temperature in El Centro varies from about 15 °C to 31 °C. In San Diego, it varies from about 14 °C to 21 °C. The more moderate temperatures in San Diego / El Centro are due to its nearness to the Pacific Ocean.

Ocean Currents

Ocean currents move water and distribute energy and nutrients around the globe. *Surface currents* are driven by prevailing winds. They carry warm water away from the equator and cool water away from the poles. Ocean currents moderate the temperatures of coastal cities. Cold ocean currents cool warmer air and warm ocean currents warm cooler air. For example, the waters of the California Current move cool water from the northern Pacific Ocean southward along the western shores of North America. This current has a general cooling effect on the air temperatures of cities near the shoreline.

17. Cool, moist air masses form over the Pacific Ocean where the cold California Current flows. Prevailing winds bring these air masses toward land. How might this process affect San Diego's climate? Explain your reasoning.

Landforms and Elevation

Landforms such as tall mountains can influence an area's climate. In some places, prevailing winds move moist air toward mountains. As the moist air rises, it cools and condenses and may cause rain or snow to fall. The air that reaches the other side of the mountain is drier, causing a rain shadow.

California has several mountain ranges that run north to south through the state. Yosemite National Park is on the western side of the Sierra Nevada mountains. Joshua Tree National Park is located to the east of California's Peninsular Ranges, which include the San Jacinto, Santa Rosa, and San Bernardino mountains. When prevailing winds carry moist air from the Pacific Ocean eastward over California, the air rises to pass over the mountains, causing wetter climates on western slopes and drier climates on eastern slopes.

Elevation also influences climate. *Elevation* is a place's distance above sea level. In a given area, as the elevation increases, the air temperature generally decreases. For example, Yosemite National Park has glacial ice at its highest elevations around 13,000 feet. It also snows at the higher elevations in the park during the winter.

18. **Write** Imagine what it would be like to walk from the California coast to the Great Basin area. Use what you have learned from the text and the diagram to describe the changes in climate during your walk.

 EVIDENCE NOTEBOOK

19. What factors influence the climates of Yosemite National Park and Joshua Tree National Park? Record your evidence.

Relate Elevation and Precipitation

Average annual precipitation varies in central California. Elevation also varies. Explore the maps to determine if and how elevation and precipitation are related in this area.

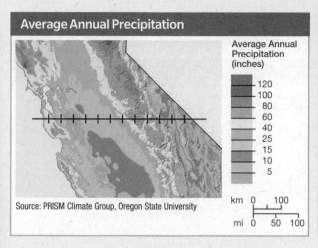

Average Annual Precipitation

Average Annual Precipitation (inches)

120
100
80
60
40
25
15
10
5

Source: PRISM Climate Group, Oregon State University

km 0   100

mi 0   50   100

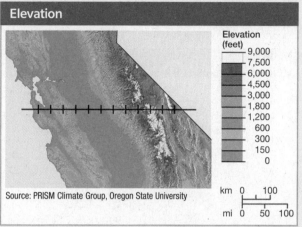

Elevation

Elevation (feet)

9,000
7,500
6,000
4,500
3,000
1,800
1,200
600
300
150
0

Source: PRISM Climate Group, Oregon State University

km 0   100

mi 0   50   100

20. Examine the lines with tick marks on each map. These marks are placed at the exact same locations on both maps. Fill in the table by estimating the elevation and precipitation at each tick mark, going from left to right.

Tick mark	1	2	3	4	5	6	7	8	9	10	11
Precipitation (in)											
Elevation (ft)											

21. Construct a graph based on the data in your table.

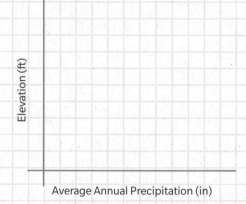

Elevation (ft)

Average Annual Precipitation (in)

22. Analyze the graph to explain the correlation between precipitation and elevation in this part of California.

Using Regional Climate Models

Climate is a complex phenomenon because it is influenced by so many factors. Models of Earth's climate types can be helpful because they make it easy to see patterns, such as latitude's effect on climate.

Earth's Climate Types

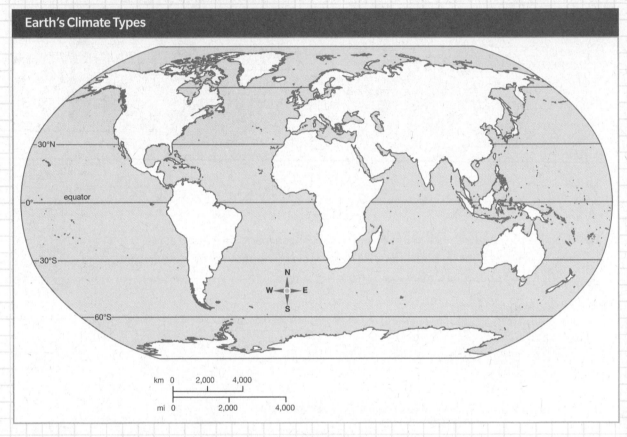

23. Divide Earth into three major climate types. Show each type on the map and include a key. Explain your reasoning for your decisions.

Earth's Regional Climates

There are several different systems used to classify climate. They can be based on different criteria, or they may represent different time periods. For example, Earth can be divided into a few major climate zones, into several regional climate types, or even into hundreds of local climates.

The Köppen-Geiger classification of regional climates is commonly used. This classification is periodically updated in order to reflect the most current data. For example, one version represents climate from 1986 to 2010. Before that version was a version that represented 1951 to 2000.

Hands-On Lab
Model Your Climate

You will develop and use a model to describe your local climate. You will use the model as a visual display in a multimedia presentation to explain the factors that influence your local climate.

Procedure and Analysis

STEP 1 Define your area of study. This might be the city you live in or a region.

STEP 2 Collect climate data for your area. Summarize the climate, including temperature and precipitation patterns. Note if there are seasons or winds, and how much and what kind of precipitation falls throughout the year.

STEP 3 Describe what factors influence your climate, or what your model's "inputs" will be. Think about sunlight, latitude, elevation, surface type, prevailing winds, landforms, and ocean currents.

STEP 4 Plan a way to model your climate. How will your model show the inputs to your local climate system?

STEP 5 How will your model show the outputs to your local climate system? For example, how will it represent temperature and precipitation outputs?

STEP 6 Identify the materials you will need to make your model.

STEP 7 Check in with a teacher to describe your plans and materials needed. Get confirmation that you are ready to proceed. Then develop your model.

STEP 8 **Language SmArts** Make a multimedia presentation to help clarify your model and emphasize your main points. Present this to the class.

Earth has several regional climates. Explore the map and photos.

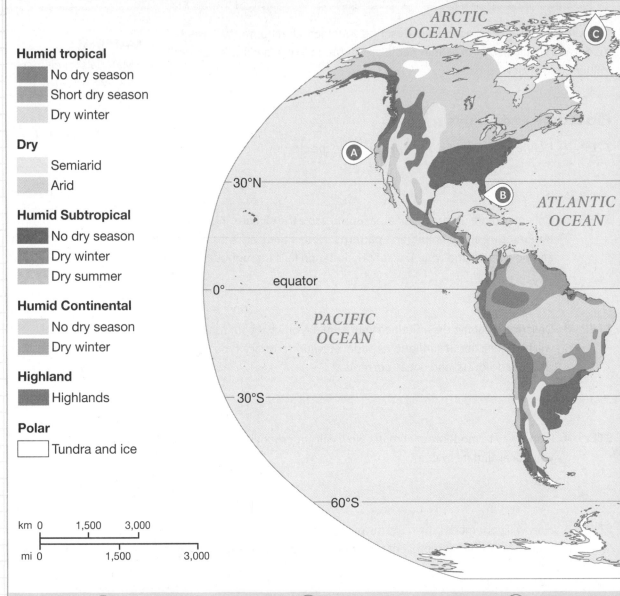

Humid tropical
- No dry season
- Short dry season
- Dry winter

Dry
- Semiarid
- Arid

Humid Subtropical
- No dry season
- Dry winter
- Dry summer

Humid Continental
- No dry season
- Dry winter

Highland
- Highlands

Polar
- Tundra and ice

ARCTIC OCEAN

ATLANTIC OCEAN

30°N

equator

0°

PACIFIC OCEAN

30°S

60°S

km 0   1,500   3,000

mi 0   1,500   3,000

The mild Mediterranean climate of coastal California is influenced by prevailing winds that bring cool, moist air in from the Pacific Ocean.

This swamp in southern Florida is located in the only tropical climate zone in the continental United States.

The arctic hares of Ellesmere Island, Canada, thrive in the polar climate of the area with its long, cold winters and brief, cool summers.

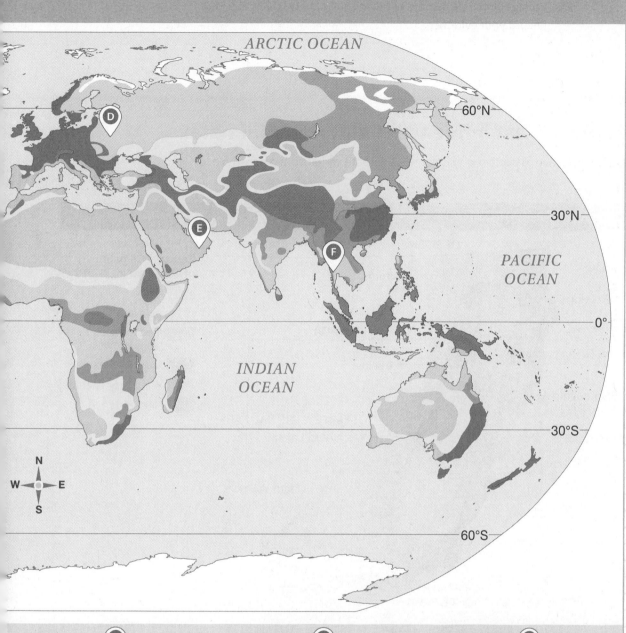

ARCTIC OCEAN

60°N

30°N

PACIFIC
OCEAN

0°

INDIAN
OCEAN

30°S

60°S

N
W ◆ E
S

Moscow, Russia, has a temperate climate with warm summers that can be somewhat humid. Winters are long and cold.

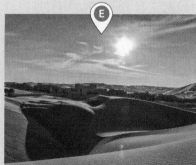

The large, hot desert of Rub' al Khali, located on the Arabian Peninsula, is the result of a high-pressure belt, high temperatures, and lack of precipitation in the arid climate.

The lush vegetation and abundant water in Erawan National Park in Thailand are the result of a humid tropical climate.

EVIDENCE NOTEBOOK

24. What regional climate types are found in the two National Parks? Record your evidence.

Explain What Influences California's Climates

Explore the map to explain why California's climate varies from place to place.

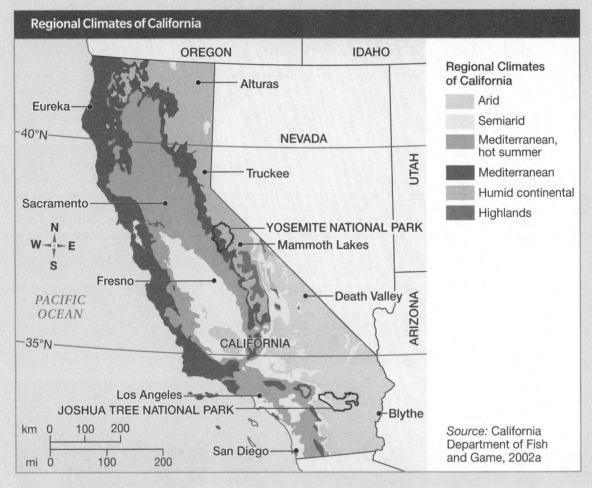

Regional Climates of California

25. Eureka and Alturas have different regional climates even though they are at a similar latitude. Part of the reason is due to nearness to Nevada / the equator / the ocean.

26. Truckee and Fresno have different climates that are mainly due to which of the following factors?

A. nearness to the Pacific Ocean

B. their latitudes

C. nearness to Nevada

D. their albedos

Continue Your Exploration

Name: _____ Date: _____

Check out the path below or go online to choose one of the other paths shown.

Exploring the Greenhouse Effect

- Lake Effect
- Hands-On Labs 🖐
- Propose Your Own Path

Go online to choose one of these other paths.

The Greenhouse Effect

How does a greenhouse work? Sunlight passes through the glass and warms the floor and objects inside. In turn, the air inside the greenhouse warms. The warm air is trapped by the glass, so the interior of the greenhouse gets warmer.

The windows in a greenhouse are similar to Earth's atmosphere. Sunlight passes through the atmosphere and warms the surface. This causes the air to warm. Some of the energy is absorbed by *greenhouse gases* in the atmosphere. This phenomenon, called the *greenhouse effect,* is what makes Earth warm enough for humans and many other plants and animals to live. However, human activities have rapidly increased the amount of greenhouse gases in the past few hundred years. This increase has caused Earth's average global temperature to rise. Rising temperatures have some negative effects on the environment, which we depend on for water, food, and other resources.

Greenhouse Gases

Naturally occurring greenhouse gases include water vapor, carbon dioxide, methane, nitrous oxide, and ozone. Human activities have caused their levels to rise. Chlorofluorocarbons (CFCs) are human-made greenhouse gases that come from using refrigerants, aerosols, and cleaning solvents.

Gases in the atmosphere retain heat, which is similar to the way a greenhouse retains heat.

Lesson 5 Earth Has Different Regional Climates **367**

Continue Your Exploration

Common Greenhouse Gases and Their Sources

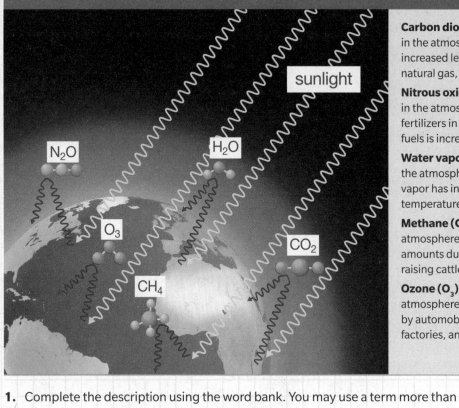

Carbon dioxide (CO_2) occurs naturally in the atmosphere, but humans have increased levels by burning coal, oil, natural gas, and wood.

Nitrous oxide (N_2O) is naturally present in the atmosphere, but human use of fertilizers in agriculture and burning fossil fuels is increasing the amount.

Water vapor (H_2O) occurs naturally in the atmosphere. The amount of water vapor has increased with increasing global temperatures.

Methane (CH_4) occurs naturally in the atmosphere, but humans have increased amounts due to oil and gas production, raising cattle, and producing garbage.

Ozone (O_3) occurs naturally in the atmosphere but can also be produced by automobile exhaust, pollution from factories, and burning vegetation.

1. Complete the description using the word bank. You may use a term more than once.

   As greenhouse gases have _____, the global average temperature has _____. Warmer global temperatures have _____ sea ice and caused sea levels to rise.

   WORD BANK
   • increased
   • decreased

2. Make an X next to the actions that would increase levels of greenhouse gases.

   _____ driving a car that burns fossil fuels

   _____ riding a bike and walking

   _____ using fertilizer to grow crops

   _____ eating less meat from cattle

3. Why do you think humans continue to do the activities that increase greenhouse gases in the atmosphere?

4. **Collaborate** Research the increase in the atmosphere's carbon dioxide concentrations over the past 100 years. Compare this to increases from previous time periods, including before humans existed. Use evidence from your research to support a conclusion about human activities and carbon dioxide in the atmosphere.

Can You Explain It?

Name: **Date:**

Why do these regions in California have such different climates?

 EVIDENCE NOTEBOOK

Refer to the notes in your Evidence Notebook to help you construct an explanation for the differences between the climates of the two locations.

1. State your claim. Make sure your claim fully explains why the climates of the two locations are so different.

2. Summarize the evidence you have gathered to support your claim and explain your reasoning.

Checkpoints

Answer the following questions to check your understanding of the lesson.

Use the graph to answer Questions 3 and 4.

3. The graph shows the average annual temperatures of four cities, which were calculated from 30 years of data. This graph therefore helps to describe each area's weather / climate.

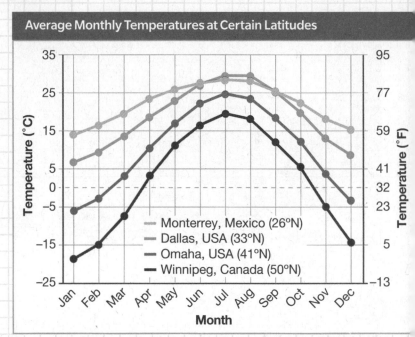

Credit: "Latitude's influence on mean monthly temperature, Figure 6.9" from Understanding Physical Geography by Michael Pidwirny. Copyright © 2014-2017 Our Planet Earth Publishing. Adapted and reproduced by permission of Our Planet Earth Publishing.

4. Look at the latitude of each city. Select all that apply.

   A. The cities at higher latitudes have less precipitation.

   B. The cities at lower latitudes are colder.

   C. The cities at lower latitudes are warmer.

   D. The cities at higher latitudes have a greater range in temperatures over the year.

5. Tobias modeled the albedo effect by laying large white and black T-shirts out in the sun. He measured the temperature / humidity of each shirt for a few hours. The end result was that the white / black shirt was warmer.

Use the map to answer Question 6.

6. London, England has mild temperatures compared to many inland cities around the same latitude. This is because warm air masses form over the warm North Atlantic Current. Prevailing winds that blow east / west to east / west bring the warm air over London.

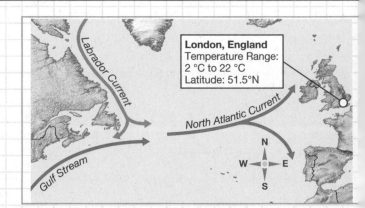

7. Snow reflects / absorbs more sunlight than water does because snow has a lower / higher albedo. As snow melts, more / less sunlight is absorbed by the darker soil beneath it. This causes cooling / warming in the local area.

Interactive Review

Complete this section to review the main concepts of the lesson.

An area's climate is described by its average temperature and precipitation patterns over a long period of time.

A. Why does describing an area's climate require weather data for more than one or two years?

Areas near the equator receive more direct sunlight than areas near the poles. Sunlight is reflected and absorbed differently by different surfaces.

B. How is climate affected by latitude?

Factors that influence climate include latitude, prevailing winds, ocean currents, elevation, surface type, and landforms.

C. Provide an example of how two or more climate factors can work together and affect California's climate.

Earth has several different regional climates.

D. Explain why regional climates do not follow latitude lines exactly.

Choose one of the activities to explore how this unit connects to other topics.

People in Science

Noelani Puniwai, Conservation Scientist Noelani Puniwai was born and raised in Puna, Hawaii. With a PhD in natural resources and environmental management, Noelani bridges the gaps between science and society to help take care of the lands and waters of Hawaii. As climate changes, Hawaii will see changes in recreation, industries, and day-to-day life of the local people. Noelani studies how surfers, fishermen, and others report and experience changes in weather patterns in Hawaii. This helps her link measurable changes in climate and weather to real-world effects.

Research the effects of climate change in Hawaii. Describe the major concerns people there are facing today. Choose one of these concerns and work with a partner to propose a solution.

Social Studies Connection

Alaskan Inuit Culture The Alaskan Inuit (uh•LAS•kuhn IN•oo•it) people inhabit many western and northern parts of Alaska. In Alaska, the average daytime winter temperature is generally below freezing. The local weather and climate have a great impact on Inuit culture.

Research the Alaskan Inuit people and how they have adapted to this cold climate. Make a multimedia presentation that includes how weather patterns influence the clothing, housing, transportation, and other lifestyle factors of the Inuit people.

Engineering Connection

Building Homes for Different Climates Architects design houses that shelter and protect people from particular environmental conditions. To design homes that are suitable for various climates, architects must understand different climates. They must also understand the types of building materials that are available and sustainable in that environment.

Research home designs and building materials architects use in different climates. Create a visual display explaining the range of materials available to construct homes in various climates and locations.

Name: _____   Date: _____

Complete this review to check your understanding of the unit.
Use the diagram to answer Questions 1 and 2.

1. What process does this image show?

   A. condensation

   B. carbon cycling

   C. convection

   D. Coriolis effect

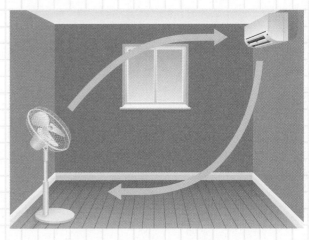

2. Which of the following is a strength of this model?

   A. Arrows are used to show movement of air.

   B. Explanations of the unseen mechanisms are included.

   C. The relationships between energy, gravity, and cycling are labeled.

   D. The model can be used to predict more processes related to air movement.

---

3. Solar energy is transformed into *electrical / magnetic / thermal* energy as the sun warms Earth's surface. Some parts of Earth are warmed more than others, so temperature differences drive convection currents in the air and oceans. As convection currents form, thermal energy is transformed into *kinetic / solar* energy.

Use the map to answer Questions 4 and 5.

4. This *weather / climate* map shows the average *type / amount* of precipitation in Colorado during the year.

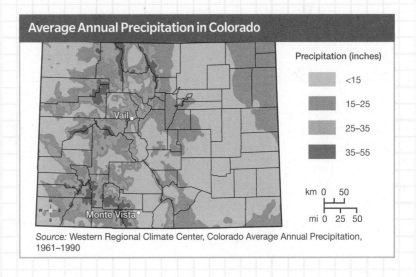

Average Annual Precipitation in Colorado

Precipitation (inches)

<15

15–25

25–35

35–55

Vail

Monte Vista

km 0   50

mi 0 25 50

Source: Western Regional Climate Center, Colorado Average Annual Precipitation, 1961–1990

5. Which of the following factors could cause the precipitation average in Vail to be higher than the precipitation average in Monte Vista?

   A. Vail is in a different county.

   B. Monte Vista is in a rain shadow.

   C. The temperature is usually hotter in Monte Vista.

   D. Monte Vista is south of Vail.

6. Complete the table by providing examples of how the factors that influence weather and climate relate to each big concept.

Factors that influence weather and climate	Cause and effect	Interactions in the Earth system	System models
Global winds	Global winds are caused by the uneven heating of Earth's surface and the rotation of Earth.		
Ocean currents			
High and low air pressure			

Name: _____   Date: _____

Use the map to answer Questions 7–9.

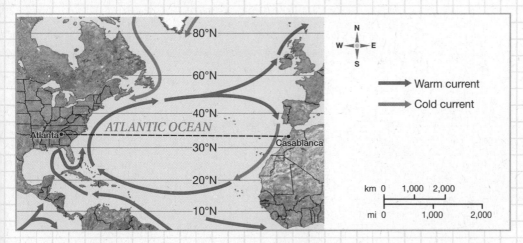

7. Atlanta has very hot and humid summers. During the fall, winter, and spring, Atlanta has milder temperatures. In Casablanca, temperatures remain mild throughout the year. Cite evidence from the map to explain why these cities have such different climates, even though they are at the same latitude.

8. Some hurricanes form near the coast of West Africa in the Atlantic Ocean, south of Casablanca. Atlanta is more likely to be affected by these hurricanes than Casablanca is. Use the map as well as your knowledge of the relationship between prevailing winds and ocean surface currents to explain why this occurs.

9. How could this map help a meteorologist make predictions about weather patterns in cities near the Atlantic Ocean? What other information might a meteorologist need to make reliable weather predictions?

Use the map to answer Questions 10–13.

Eria, an Imaginary Continent on Earth

Examine this map of an imaginary continent to explain weather and climate patterns.

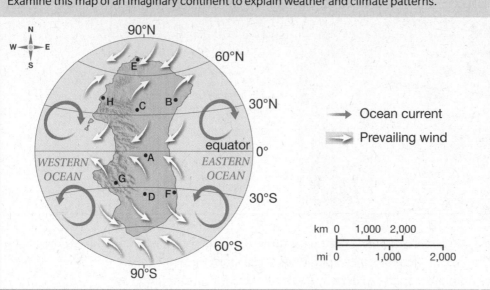

10. What factors are represented on this map that could potentially affect weather and climate on the continent?

11. Identify the location where you would most likely find a rain forest. Support your claim with evidence and reasoning.

12. The Eastern Ocean is warm between 0° and 30°S. What type of air mass likely forms here? How might this affect point A, which is at a low elevation?

13. Why might the climate in location H be different from the climate in location C?

Name: _____   Date: _____

What Influences Marine Layers in California?

Have you ever heard of "May Gray" or "June Gloom"? In certain locations in California, cool mornings filled with heavy clouds and fog are common during these months. This is due to the formation of a *marine layer*. Sometimes, you can travel to an elevation above the marine layer and experience warmer and sunnier weather!

You will collect data to describe how marine layers form, identify where they form, and note the climate types associated with them. You will explain why only certain locations experience marine layers and then explain the effects of marine layers on people and other living things.

The steps below will help guide you in planning an investigation and constructing an explanation.

1. **Ask Questions** Develop a list of questions about the marine layer that develops in California.

2. **Conduct Research** Find information about marine layers that develop in California and describe their effect on weather. Where specifically in California do they form? Describe what influences the development of marine layers, including any local factors and global weather patterns. List other places in the world where marine layers develop and note the climate types associated with each location.

3. **Analyze Data** Compare locations and climate types where marine layers form in the world. Describe any patterns you notice.

4. **Construct an Explanation** Explain why some coastal cities in California experience "May Gray" and "June Gloom" while others do not. Use evidence from your research to support your answer.

5. **Construct an Explanation** Explain how weather associated with marine layers affects people and other living things. Use evidence from your research to support your explanations.

✓ **Self-Check**

	I described both the local factors and global weather patterns that influence the development of marine layers in California.
	I described the weather associated with marine layers and identified where marine layers develop in California.
	I compared locations and climate types where marine layers develop around the world.
	I provided evidence to explain why only certain locations are affected by marine layers.
	I provided evidence to explain how marine layers could affect people and other living things.

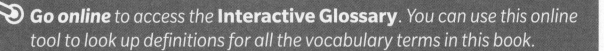

*Go online to access the **Interactive Glossary**. You can use this online tool to look up definitions for all the vocabulary terms in this book.*

Pronunciation Key

Sound	Symbol	Example	Respelling	Sound	Symbol	Example	Respelling
ă	a	pat	PAT	ŏ	ah	bottle	BAHT'l
ā	ay	pay	PAY	ō	oh	toe	TOH
âr	air	care	KAIR	ô	aw	caught	KAWT
ä	ah	father	FAH•ther	ôr	ohr	roar	ROHR
är	ar	argue	AR•gyoo	oi	oy	noisy	NOYZ•ee
ch	ch	chase	CHAYS	o͞o	u	book	BUK
ĕ	e	pet	PET	o͞o	oo	boot	BOOT
ĕ (at end of a syllable)	eh	settee lessee	seh•TEE leh•SEE	ou	ow	pound	POWND
ĕr	ehr	merry	MEHR•ee	s	s	center	SEN•ter
ē	ee	beach	BEECH	sh	sh	cache	CASH
g	g	gas	GAS	ŭ	uh	flood	FLUHD
ĭ	i	pit	PIT	ûr	er	bird	BERD
ĭ (at end of a syllable)	ih	guitar	gih•TAR	z	z	xylophone	ZY•luh•fohn
ī	y eye (only for a complete syllable)	pie island	PY. EYE•luhnd	z	z	bags	BAGZ
îr	ir	hear	HIR	zh	zh	decision	dih•SIZH•uhn
j	j	germ	JERM	ə	uh	around broken focus	uh•ROWND BROH•kuhn FOH•kuhs
k	k	kick	KIK	ər	er	winner	WIN•er
ng	ng	thing	THING	th	th	thin they	THIN THAY
ngk	ngk	bank	BANGK	w	w	one	WUHN
				wh	hw	whether	HWETH•er

Index

Page numbers for key terms are in **boldface** type.
Page numbers in *italic* type indicate illustrative material, such as photographs, graphs, charts, and maps.

E

ear, 149, 153

Earth
absorbing and reflecting sunlight, 354, *354*, 511, *511*
albedo, 356–357
changes in orbit of, 515, 516
climates of, 350–366, *362*, *364–365*, 371, 384, *384*
diversity of living things on, 418
satellites orbiting, 85
surface changes of, 516
surface temperature changes, 520, *520*

Earth Science Connection
Climate and Reproduction, 478

Earth's rotation
causing winds and air currents, 98
Coriolis effect, 276, *276*
effect on gyres patterns, 292–293, *293*
effect on pressure systems, 317, *317*
jet streams caused by, 283, *283*
matter in atmosphere effected by, 275

Earth System
air circulation relating to, 279–282
air movement patterns in atmosphere of, 268–287
air pressure in, 314, *314*
analyzing water on, 238–240
carbon cycle on, *304*
climate system, 511–513
cycling of matter in, 303
energy flow in, 174
ice on surface of, 248, *248*
interaction in, 89, 310–327, 511
modeling of, 97–102
movement of water on, 245–246, 288–305
states of water on, 239–240
subsystems of, 97–102, *97*, *270*, *300*

Eastern gray squirrel, 458, *458*

E. coli bacteria, 93, *93*

economy, 100

ecosystem, 534
biodiversity of, 535, 551
climate change disrupting, 538
dam system disrupting, 247
habitat degradation, 542
health of, 534–535
importance of, 544
levels of, 534, *534*
roads affecting, 16

Eco-Task Force, 483

Edison, Thomas, 44, 57

egg
of aggregating anemone, 461, *461*
of birds, 459, *459*, 464
of dragonflies, 458
of fish, 420, *420*, 459, *459*, 553, *553*
of flowering plants, 441
of octopus, 464
parents protecting, 464
of seedless plants, 437, *437*
of seed plants, 438

elastic potential energy, 181

electrical current, 182

electrical energy
defined, 181–182
reducing use of, 570, *570*
sensory response, 153
from steam turbines, 567, *567*
transformation of, 190, *190*

electrical engineer, 73–74

electric circuits in computers, 14

electromagnetic energy, 181, 190, *190*, 219

electromagnetic receptor, 154

electron microscope, 111

elephant, 419, 456, *456*

elephant seal, 462

elevation, 360, 361, *361*, 371, 385, *385*

elk, 463, *463*, 535

Ellesmere Island, Canada, 364, *364*

El Niño, 518, *518*, 539

embryo
of fish, 118, *118*
of mollusk, 458
of plants, 438, 446

Emperor penguin, 383, 397, *397*

endoplasmic reticulum, 116, *116*, 117, *117*

endoskeleton, 149

endosymbiosis, 123

energy
causing changes, 178
clouds absorbing, 313
collision transferring, 186–187
convection transferring, 300–301
Earth balancing, 354, *354*, 511, *511*
in Earth systems, 97
flowing and causing change, 176–196
flow of in atmosphere, 281, 287
flow of in oceans, 303, 309
flow of in systems, 173–264
flow of water cycle, 251
forms of, 181–182
gravitational potential energy, 180–181
hydroelectric power station transforming, 176
identifying forms of, 178–183
kinetic, 178–179
law of conservation of energy, 180
loss in systems, 191–192
mechanical energy, 181–182
modeling transformation of, 189–192
moving through biosphere, 99
observing transfer of, 184–188
from photosynthesis, 90, 130
potential energy, 180–181
in radiometer, 218
stored, 180–181
from sun, 98, 303
surface wind and surface current transferring, 292
in systems, 90
thermal energy, 98, 189
transfers of within a system, 90, 178
in water cycle, 98
from wind, 39–40

energy conservationist, 231–232

energy drive, in water cycle, 236–257

energy efficient, 192

energy-efficient appliance, 563

energy-efficient home, 232, *232*

F

fertilization, 425, 437, *437*, 459
fertilizer, 557
fibrous root, 134, *134*
filament, 57
fire
  in homes, 28–30
  wildfire, *99, 99, 270, 270,* 539
  winds moving, 279
fireworks, 190, *190*, 197, *197*
fish
  in coral reef, 90, *90*
  embryo cell of, 118, *118*
  reproduction of, 420, 458, *458*
Fisher, Paul, 70
flagella, 115, *115*
flashlight, 178
floating garbage, 289, *289,* 303, 307,
    307, 485, *485*
flood, 491
flood control, 500, *500*
floragraph, 104, *104*
Florida climate, 364, *364*
Florida panther, 496–497, *496–497*
flow chart, *560*
flower, 131, *131*
flowering seed plant, 437, 441–445
fog
  formation of, 223, *223,* 324
  in San Francisco, 223, *223,* 265, *265*
food
  cooking process, 28–29
  cooking with solar energy, 173
  plants producing, 133
  storage of, 9
  in systems, 90
food web, 334, *334,* 535
force
  of air pressure, 314
  kinetic energy started by, 178, *178*
Ford, Henry, 68
forecasters, 333, 341
forest
  California land cover, 387
  plants in, 130
formation of hail, 244
formula
  cricket chirps, 339, *339*
  density, 295
  relative humidity, 312, 313, *313*

stomatal percentage, *137*
surface area-to-volume ratio, 121
thermal conductivity, 210, 224
trend lines, 336, *336*
fossil, 514, *514*
fossil fuel, 191, *304,* 496, 519, 523,
    531, *531,* 538
fox, *535*
Franklin, Rosalind, 411–412, *412*
Franz Josef Glacier, 527, *527*
fresh water, density of, 295
Fresno, California, 366, *366*
frilled lizard, 96, *96*
frog, 148, *148,* 433, *433,* 462
frontal lobe, 155, *155*
front of weather, 319–32
frozen water, 98, *98*
fruit, 436, *436*
full clone, 419
function
  of cell structures, 115–118
  structure related to, 19–20
  of tissue, 94
fungal infection, 417, *417*
fungi
  decomposition by, 99
  multicellular organism, 110, 430
  sexual and asexual reproduction of,
    420, 425, 430
  on whitebark pine, 483, *483*
furnace, 567, *567*

G

gamete, 425
garbage, oceans cycling, 303
gases
  sound energy vibrating particles of,
    182
  state of water, 239, *239,* 257
  thermal energy's relationship to,
    221
gas lamp, 32
gene, 404
  differences in, 446
  location of, 408, *408*
  modeling, 406–407
  mutation of, 419

passed from parent to offspring,
    408–409
  traits influenced by, 404–407, 415
generator, 191
genetic, 459
genetic material
  in asexual reproduction, 419, 423–
    424, *424,* 433, 460
  in DNA, 405, *405,* 415
  information for cell function, 115,
    115
  organisms influenced by, 379–484
  passed from parent to offspring,
    408–409
  in plant cells, 130
  reproduction passing down, 418
  in sexual reproduction, 419, 425,
    425, 433
  variation in, 425, 428, 437, 459, *459*
  in zygote, 425
genetics
  animal growth affected by, 466–467
  animals affected by, 456–473, 477
  disease caused by, 407, 466
  diversity of, 416–428, 455
  plants affected by, 434–450, 455
  structures of, 404–407
genotype, 406, 409, *409,* 426–427
geosphere, 97, *97,* 98, 300, 495, 511
geothermal heat pumps, 230, *230*
germination, 446
ghost pepper, 451, *451*
giant mirror, 207, *207*
giant sequoia tree, 130
gill, 148
giraffe, 391, *391*
glacier, 98, 248, *248,* 514, *514,* 516,
    516, 538, *538*
glassware, 7
Glen Canyon Dam, 247
global circulation pattern, 301, *301*
global climate, 510, *510*
global climate change, 485–582
  biodiversity, 543
  causes of, 514–519
  monitoring organism, 545–546, 551
  organisms responding, 538–543,
    549

Q

R